DICTI

INTERACTION OF COLOR FOR DESIGN

Editorial Dimai·Studio

PUBLISHED BY: Editorial Dimai Studio

Introduction

This second volume continues our two-part exploration of color, inviting you to dive deeper into a fresh set of over 70 hues. Each shade has been handpicked to expand your palette library, offering new avenues for creative expression. Like its companion, this guide stands alone—feel free to use it on its own or side-by-side with Volume I to tailor your work with both versatility and coherence.

Fundamentals of Color Combinations

1. Why These Palettes Matter

Spanning pages 9 – 204, this volume showcases 70 individual swatches grouped into seven core families—Reds & Warm Tones, Pinks & Mauves, Browns & Earths, Yellows & Oranges, Greens, Blues & Teals, and Neutrals & Fundamentals—and delivers hundreds of ready-to-use two-, three-, and four-color combinations to jump-start any creative project.

- **Pairs (Bicombinations)**

Rely on bold complements or gentle analogues to set the tone—perfect for logos or call-out graphics.

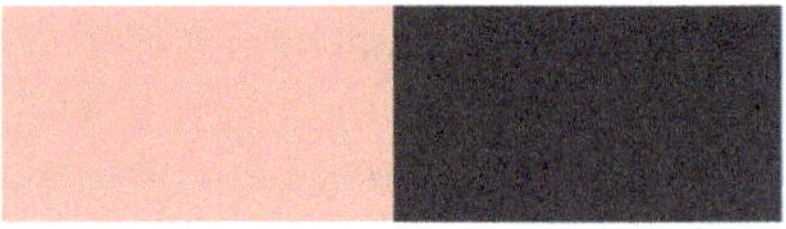

Rose Quartz Jet Black

- **Triads**

Three equidistant hues create a stable yet lively balance, ideal for multi-layered designs.

Pale Burnt Lake Salmon Diamine Green

- **Tetrads**

Two complementary pairs or rectangular arrangements deliver complexity, suited for sophisticated branding or detailed illustrations.

Vistoris Lake Mint Green

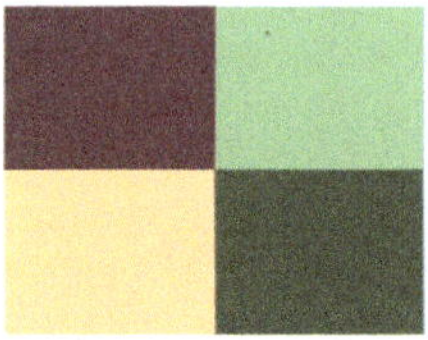

Peach Lincoln Green

3. Understanding Color Properties

Every primary swatch includes digital codes so you can reproduce it precisely:

- **Hue:** The basic tint that names each color (e.g., Etruscan Red vs. Laelia Pink).
- **Value:** Lightness or darkness, guiding contrast and depth.
- **Chroma (Saturation):** Intensity level, from muted to vivid.
- **RGB & Hex Codes:** ready for web, app, or digital design.

Names evoke history, nature, and emotion—think Venetian reds, autumnal ochres, forest greens, and twilight blues.

4. Applying These Palettes

Brand Identity & Marketing: Jump-start your color toolkit with curated systems for logos, packaging, and digital campaigns.

- **Editorial & Illustration:** Establish hierarchy and ambiance with palettes that guide the eye.

- **Fashion & Interiors:** coordinated color stories for fabrics, furnishings, and environments.

- **Cinematic & Photographic Storytelling:** color

5. Why Volume II Matters

- **Expanded Range:** A fresh set of 70 hues brings new possibilities beyond Volume I's palette.
- **Compact & Handy:** The pocket-sized format moves with you—perfect for client meetings, photo shoots, or on-site design reviews.
- **Theory in Practice:** Instead of dry diagrams, you get ready-made combinations backed by real-world testing.

Use Volume II as your color compass: each spread is an invitation to explore hue, value, and saturation in new contexts, turning your creative visions into vibrant realities.

TABLE OF CONTENTS

09 Burgundy
11 Pale Burnt Lake
14 Royal Red
18 Crimson Color
20 Etruscan Red
23 Fresh Color
25 Hydrangea Red
27 Amaranth
29 Indian Lake
31 Amaranth Purple
33 Rose Quartz
37 Laelia Pink
39 Fawn
41 Light Mauve
44 Grayish Lavender
47 Amethyst
49 Violet Red
51 Ucla Blue

Dark Slate Purple 53
Dusky Madder V 55
Vandyke Brown 58
Vistoris Lake 61
Taupe Brown 64
Tile Color 67
Corn Snake 70
Vermilion 72
Cinnamon Rufous 74
Orange Citrine 77
Isabella Color 79
Fallow Color 81
Ivory 83
Wheat 88
Pumpkin Color 90
Chocolate 94
Light Naples Yellow 96
Mustard Yellow 99

102 Pyrite Yellow
104 Sulphine Yellow
107 Olive Ocher
110 Light Green Yellow
112 Malachite
114 Avocado Green
116 Olive Buff
118 Buffy Citrine
120 Dark Citrine
122 Moss Green
124 Rainette Green
126 Eton Blue
128 Jade
130 Emerald Green
132 Pine Green
136 Cossack Green
139 British Racing Green
142 Greyish Beige

Army Green 144
Coffee 146
Slate Green 149
Laurel Green 152
Aquamarine 154
Pastel Blue 158
Peacock Blue 162
Antwarp Blue 164
Royal Blue 168
Navy Blue 171
Duke Blue 175
Dark Blue 178
White 181
Beige 183
Neutral Gray 188
Jet Black 192
Black 196

BURGUNDY

#800020

RGB : 128. 0. 32

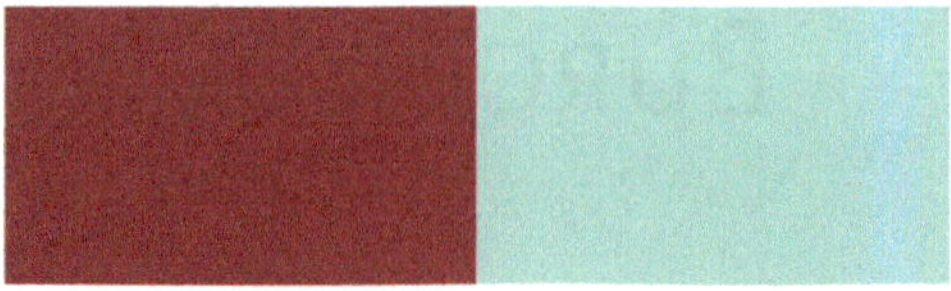

BURGUNDY AQUAMARINE

BURGUNDY SEA GREEN CHARTREUSE

BURGUNDY CHERRY TURQUOISE GREEN

BURGUNDY AUBERGINE PURPLE

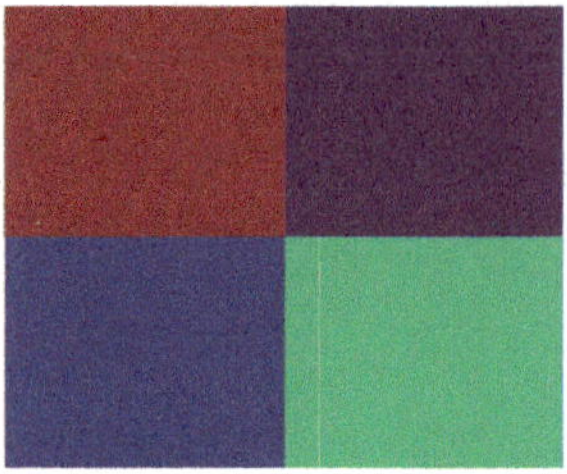

VIOLET EMERALD GREEN

BURGUNDY JET BLACK

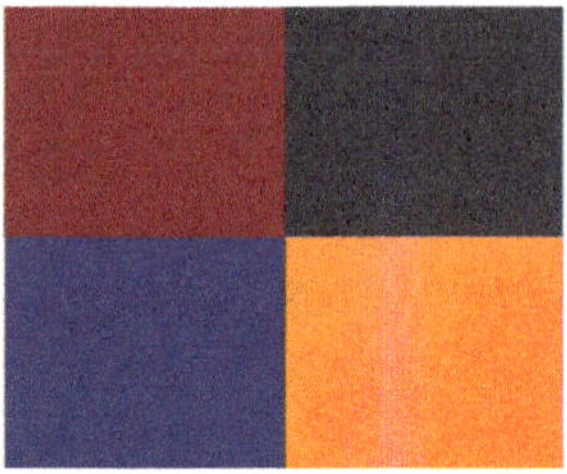

VIOLET PUMPKIN COLOR

Pale Burnt Lake

#6B2627

RGB : 107. 38. 39

Pale Burnt Lake | Olive Yellow | Yellow Ocher

Pale Burnt Lake | Pumpkin Color | Glaucous Green

Pale Burnt Lake | Buffy Citrine | Grayish Lavender

Pale Burnt Lake | Vinaceous Cinnamon | Violet

Pale Burnt Lake Salmon Diamine Green

Pale Burnt Lake Olive

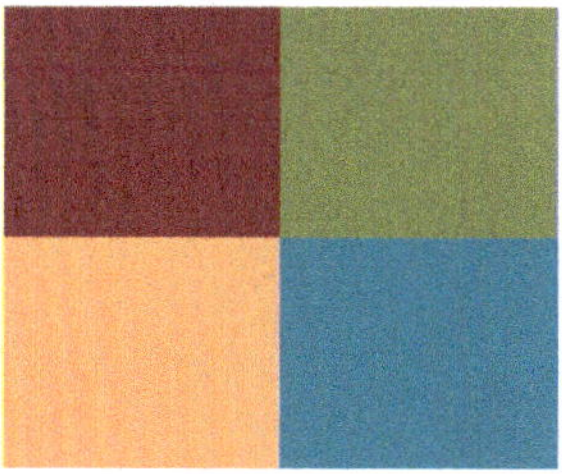

Middle Yellow Red Antwarp Blue

Pale Burnt Lake Black

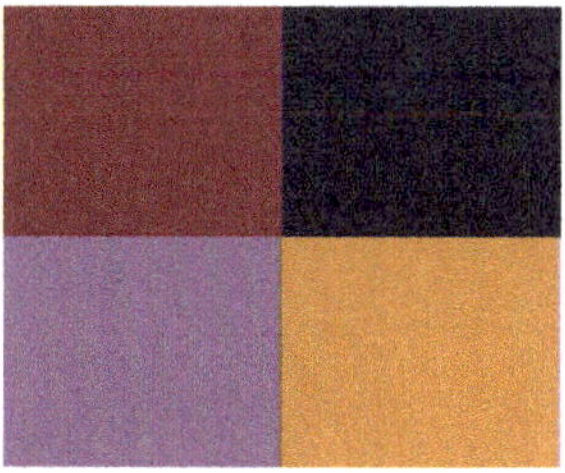

Aconite Violet Bronze

Pale Burnt Lake Amaranth

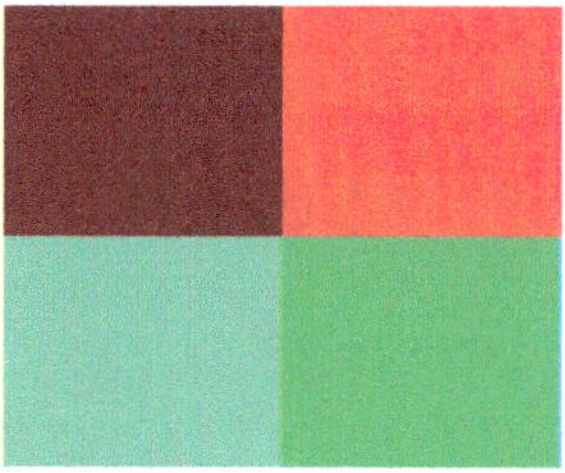

Venice Green Jade

Royal Red

#9B1C31

RGB : 155. 28. 49

ROYAL RED THISTLE

ROYAL RED BLUE

ROYAL RED BEIGE

ROYAL RED VIOLET BRONZE

Royal Red | Cotinga Purple | Violet

Royal Red | Olive Buff | Jade

Royal Red | Black | Neutral Gray

Royal Red | Neutral Gray | Peach

Royal Red | Violet Blue | Buffy Citrine

Royal Red | Alice Blue | Madder Brown

Royal Red | Pistachio

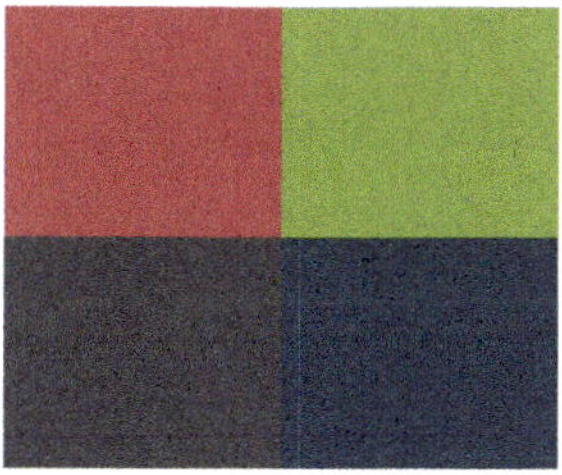

Jet Black | Dark Blue

Royal Red | Gold

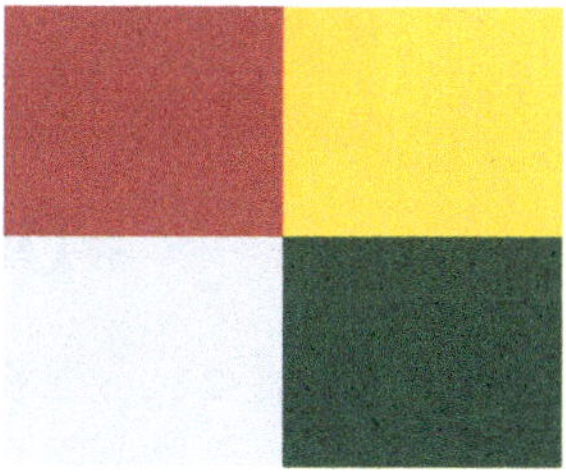

Lavender | British Racing Green

Crimson Color

#DC143C

RGB: 220. 20. 60

CRIMSON COLOR SEA GREEN

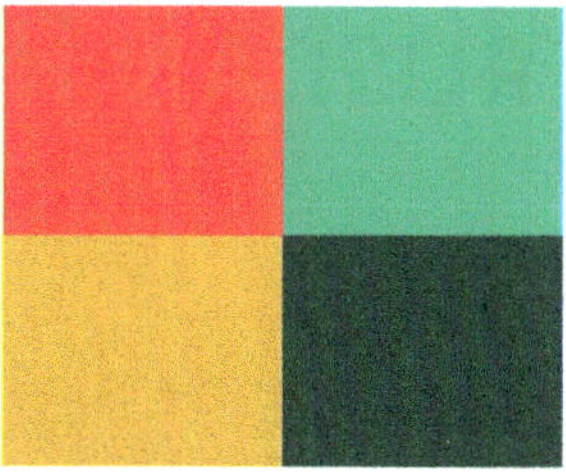

MUSTARD YELLOW BRITISH RACING GREEN

Etruscan Red

#CB7F68

RGB : 203. 127. 104

ETRUSCAN RED | NILE BLUE

ETRUSCAN RED | LAVENDER

ETRUSCAN RED | ROSE QUARTZ

ETRUSCAN RED | PETROL GREEN | CINNAMON BUFF

ETRUSCAN RED | PASTEL BLUE | CUTTLEFISH

ETRUSCAN RED | PEACH | THISTLE

ETRUSCAN RED | PEARL WHITE

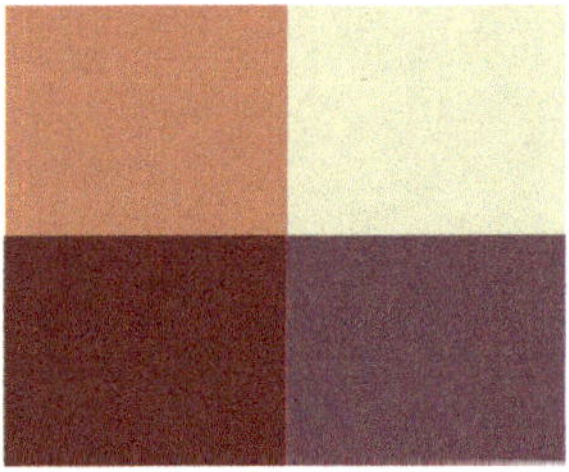

MADDER BROWN | TAUPE BROWN

Fresh Color

#E98A77

RGB : 233. 138. 119

FRESH COLOR | CADET BLUE | YELLOW

HYDRANGEA RED

#963D4A

RGB : 150. 61. 74

HYDRANGEA RED | ALICE BLUE | SULPHINE YELLOW

Amaranth

#E52B50

RGB : 229. 43. 80

AMARANTH NAVY BLUE GREYISH BEIGE

AMARANTH JADE

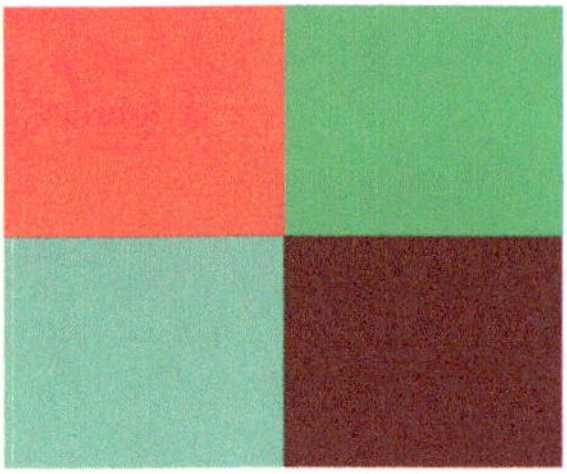

VENICE GREEN PALE BURNT LAKE

Indian Lake

#B43A5E

RGB : 180. 58. 94

Indian Lake | Pistachio

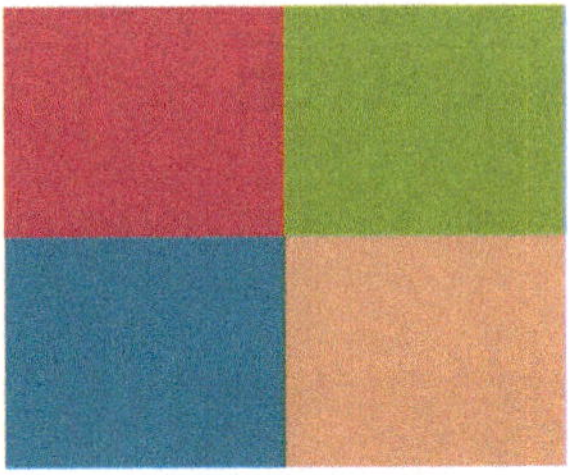

Antwarp Blue | Vinaceous Cinnamon

Indian Lake | Light Mauve

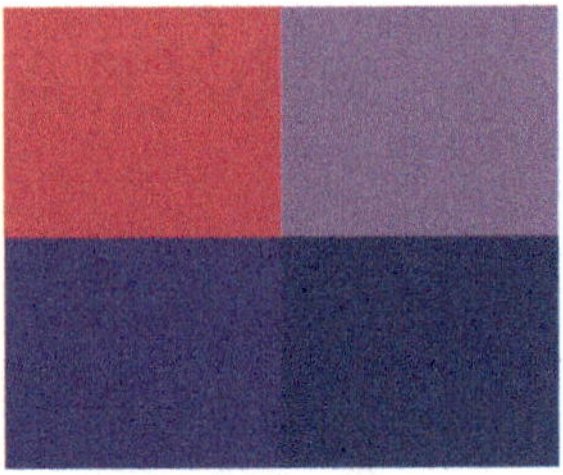

Violet | Might Night Blue

Amaranth Purple

#AB274F

RGB : 171. 39. 79

AMARANTH PURPLE ACONITE VIOLET SALMON

AMARANTH PURPLE MINT GREEN

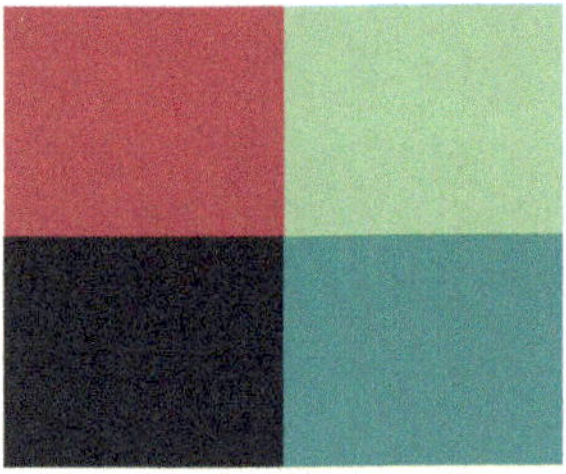

DARK GREEN CYAN GREEN BLUE

Rose Quartz

#F7CAC9

RGB: 247. 202. 201

Rose Quartz Jet Black

Rose Quartz Aconite Violet

Rose Quartz Citron Yellow

Rose Quartz Etruscan Red

ROSE QUARTZ LIGHT MAUVE VENICE GREEN

ROSE QUARTZ GRAY PEACH

ROSE QUARTZ TAUPE BROWN LAVENDER

ROSE QUARTZ CINNAMON RUFOUS PERSIAN ORANGE

Rose Quartz | Tile Color

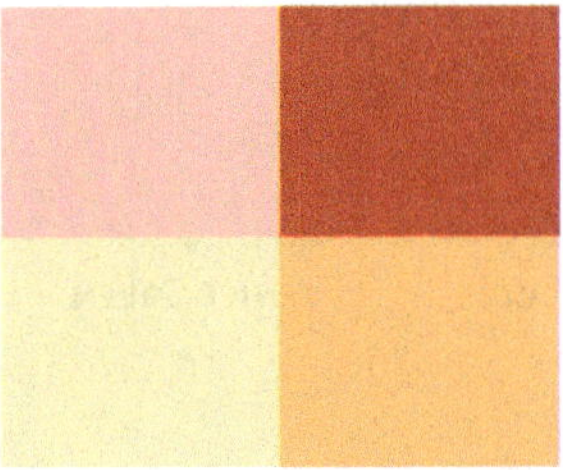

Beige | Cinnamon Buff

Rose Quartz | Olive

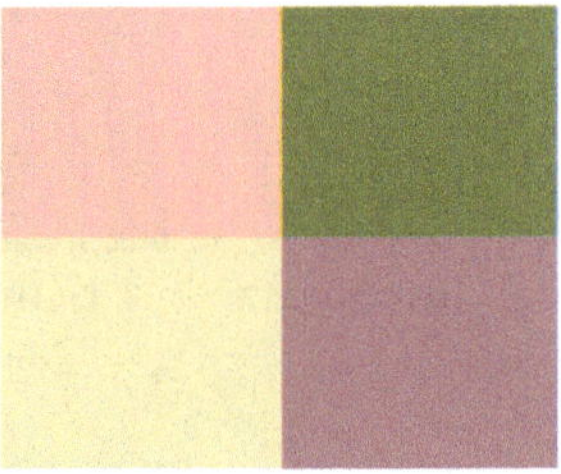

Beige | Laelia Pink

Rose Quartz | Cadet Blue

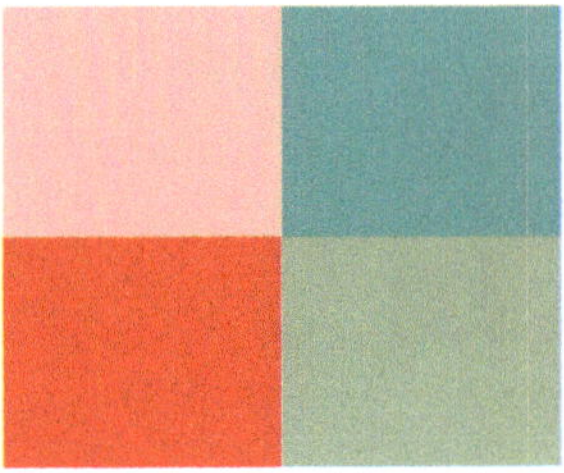

Red Orange | Laurel Green

Rose Quartz | Slate Green

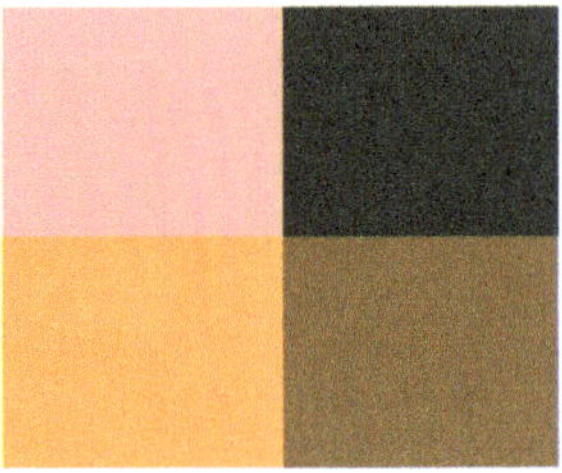

Cream Yellow | Orange Citrine

Laelia Pink

#BD8A9B

RGB : 189. 138. 155

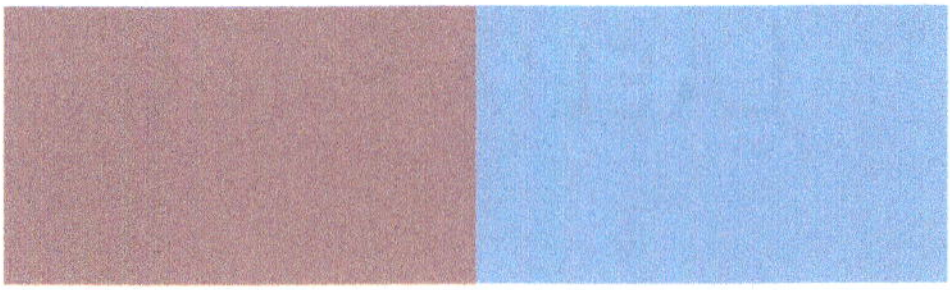

LAELIA PINK LIGHT BLUE

LAELIA PINK OLIVE

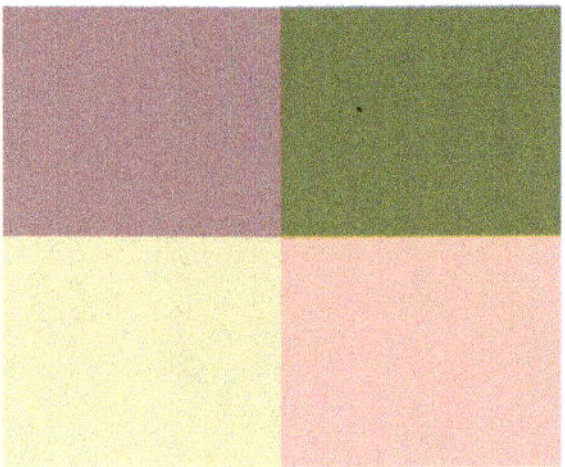

BEIGE ROSE QUARTZ

LAELIA PINK OLD RED

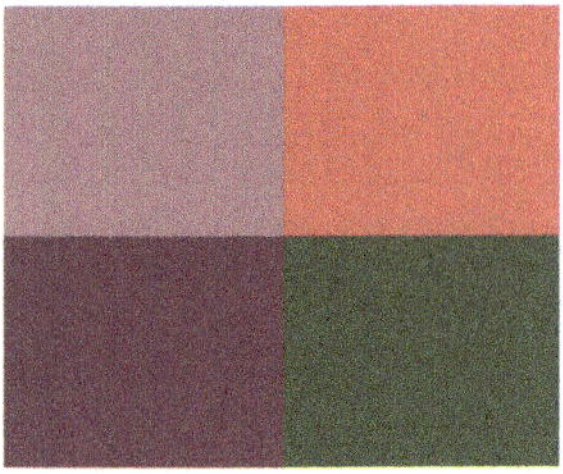

TAUPE BROWN LINCOLN GREEN

LAELIA PINK VIOLET CARMINE

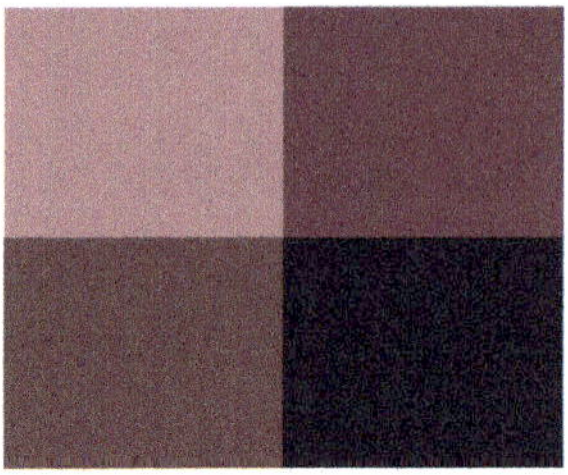

VISTORIS LAKE BLACK

Fawn

#C7A99D

RGB : 199. 169. 157

Fawn Dusky Madder Violet

Fawn Cadet Blue Violet Blue

Fawn Vermilion

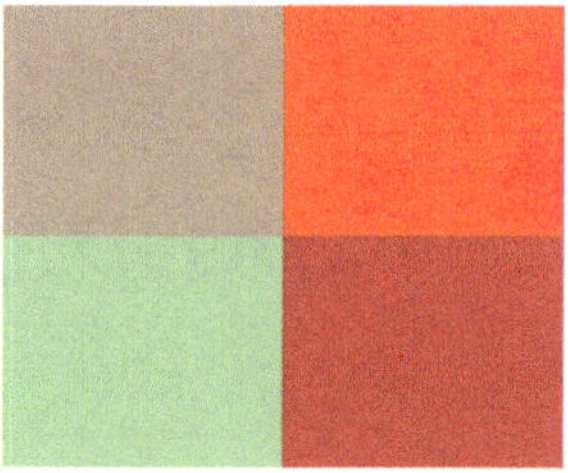

Mint Green Upsdell Red

Light Mauve

#8F6A99

RGB : 143. 106. 153

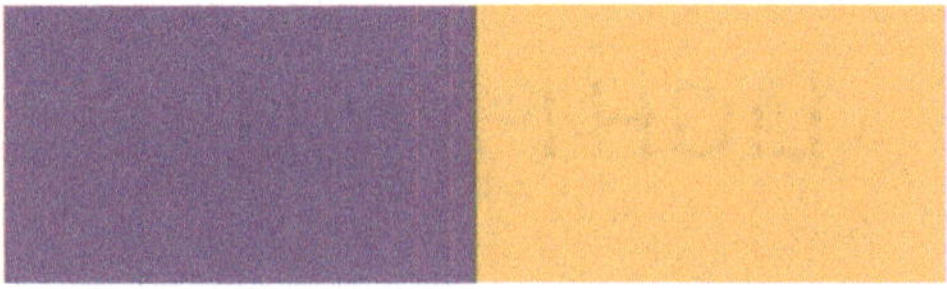

LIGHT MAUVE | CINNAMON BUFF

LIGHT MAUVE | BEIGE

LIGHT MAUVE | VENICE GREEN | ROSE QUARTZ

LIGHT MAUVE | EOSINE PINK | AUBERGINE PURPLE

LIGHT MAUVE NEUTRAL GRAY CINNAMON BUFF

LIGHT MAUVE ALMAGRE

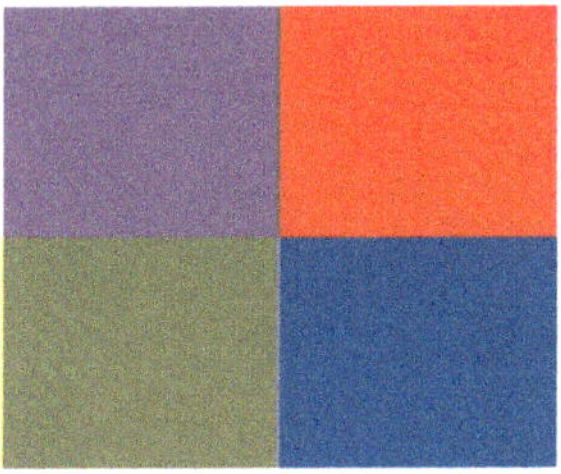

DARK CITRINE INDIGO BLUE

LIGHT MAUVE INDIAN LAKE

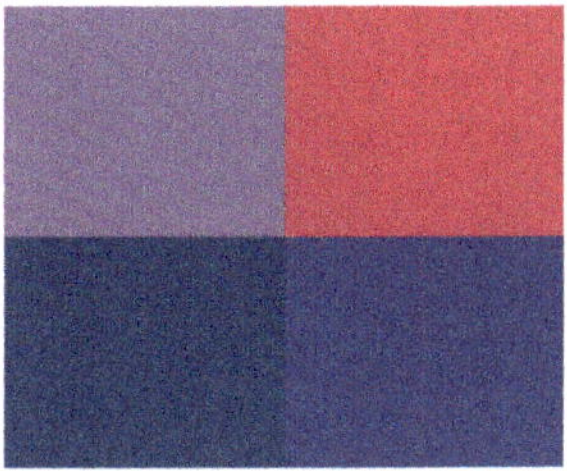

MIGHT NIGHT BLUE VIOLET

Grayish Lavender

#AEA9C8

RGB : 174. 169. 200

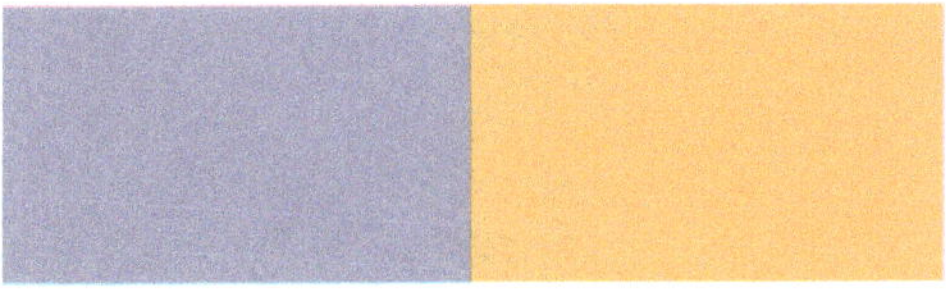

GRAYISH LAVENDER | CINNAMON RUFOUS

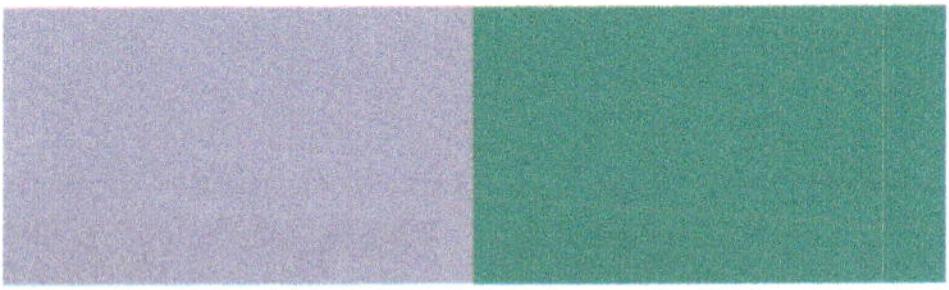

GRAYISH LAVENDER | PINE GREEN

GRAYISH LAVENDER | KHAKI | LIGHT BLUE

GRAYISH LAVENDER | BUFFY CITRINE | PALE BURNT LAKE

GRAYISH LAVENDER ROYAL BLUE UCLA BLUE

GRAYISH LAVENDER KHAKI

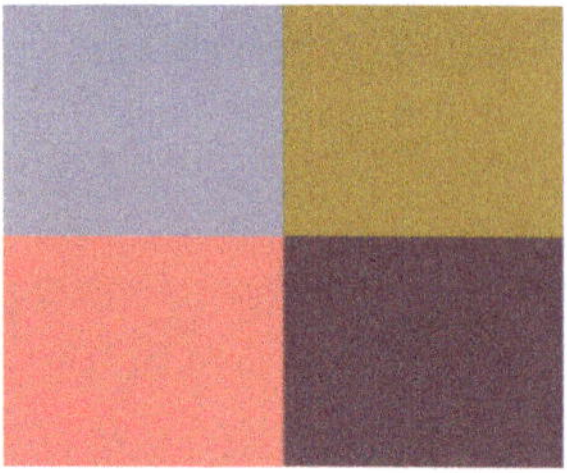

EOSINE PINK DARK SLATE PURPLE

GRAYISH LAVENDER RASPBERRY RED

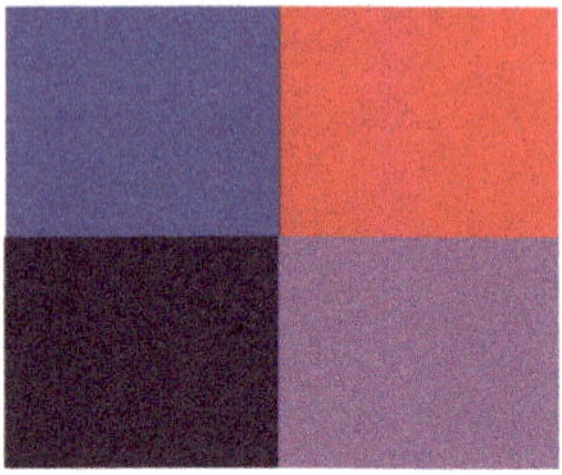

COTINGA PURPLE ACONITE VIOLET

Amethyst

#898AC0

RGB: 137. 138. 192

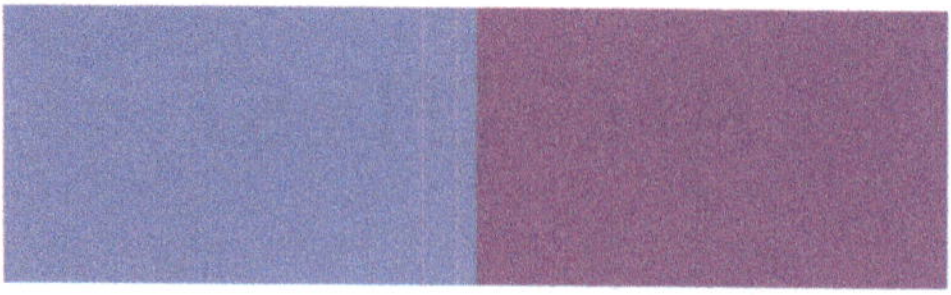

Amethyst   Aconite Violet

Amethyst   Cinnamon Buff   Petrol Green

Amethyst   Eosine Pink   Neutral Gray

Violet Red

#3D0079

RGB : 61. 0. 121

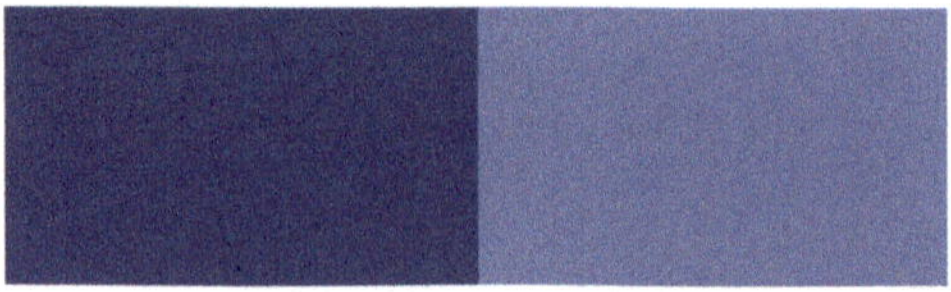

VIOLET RED SAPPHIRE

Ucla Blue

#536895

RGB : 83. 104. 149

UCLA BLUE AUBERGINE PURPLE DEEP RUBY

UCLA BLUE VANDYKE BROWN CREAM YELLOW

UCLA BLUE GRAYISH LAVENDER ROYAL BLUE

Dark Slate Purple

#633E4C

RGB : 99. 62. 76

Dark Slate Purple Raspberry Red British Racing Green

Dark Slate Purple Khaki

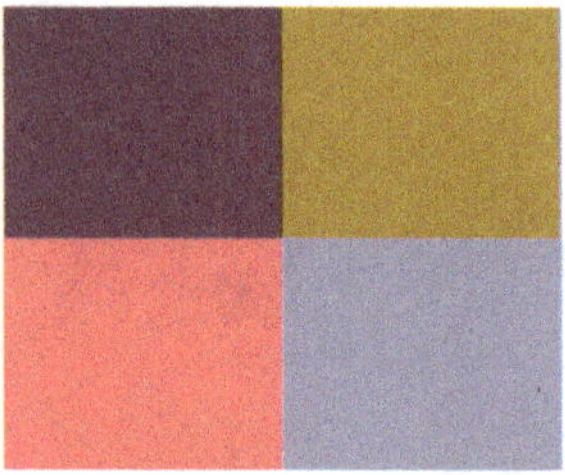

Eosine Pink Grayish Lavender

Dusky Madder Violet

#3B1C38

RGB : 59. 28. 56

Dusky Madder Violet | Fawn

Dusky Madder Violet | Ivory

Dusky Madder Violet | Pumpkin Color

Dusky Madder Violet | Cuttlefish

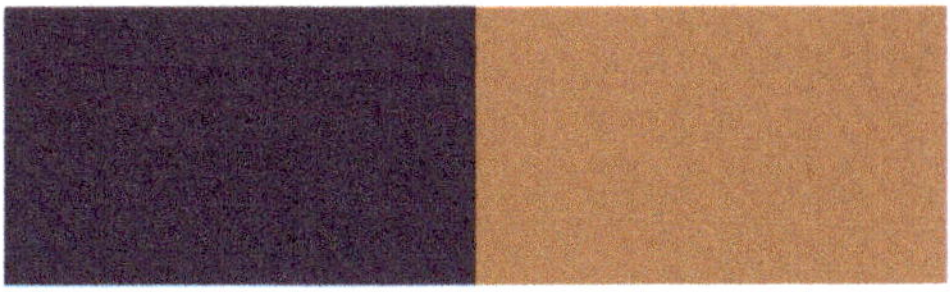

DUSKY MADDER VIOLET CINNAMON RUFOUS

DUSKY MADDER VIOLET EOSINE PINK

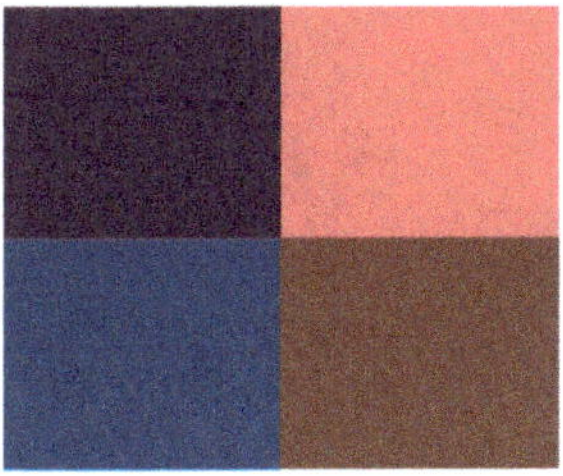

NAVY BLUE CUTTLEFISH

Vandyke Brown

#3E2F1D

RGB : 62. 47. 29

Vandyke Brown | Brown

Vandyke Brown | PapayaWhip

Vandyke Brown | Yellow Ocher

VANDYKE BROWN BRONZE DEEP INDIGO

VANDYKE BROWN CREAM YELLOW UCLA BLUE

VANDYKE BROWN TILE COLOR

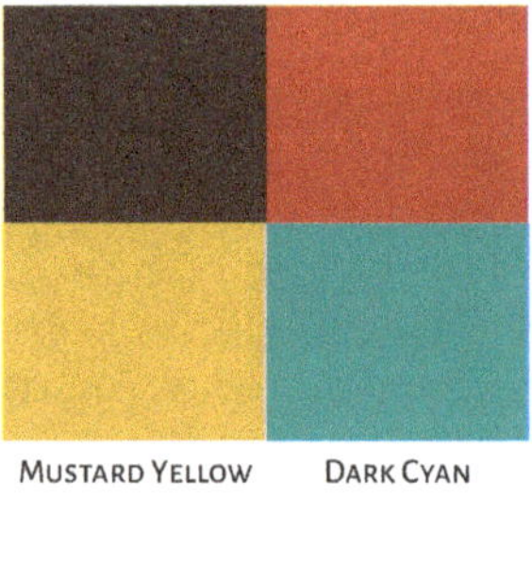

MUSTARD YELLOW DARK CYAN

VISTORIS LAKE

#5E3B3D

RGB : 94. 59. 61

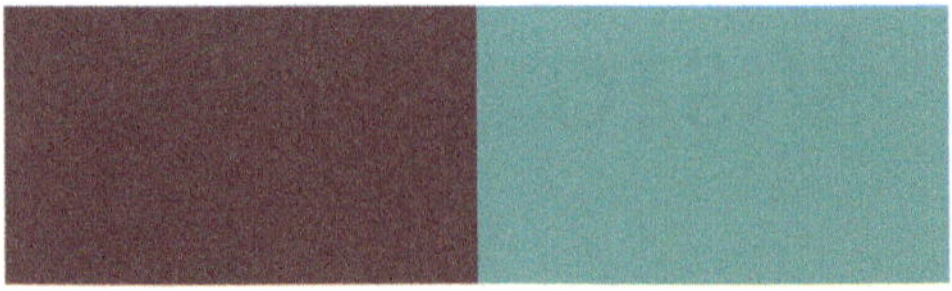

VISTORIS LAKE | CADET BLUE

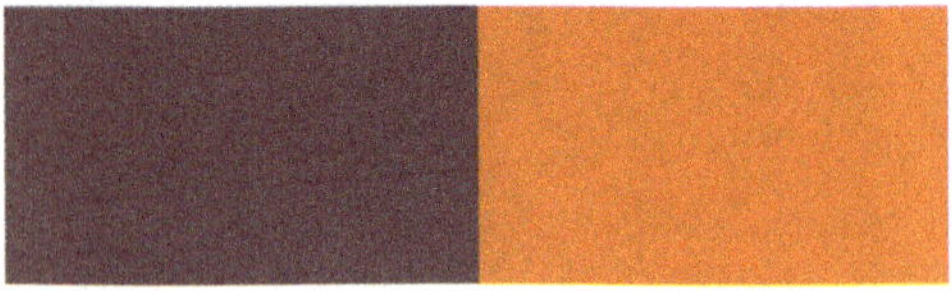

VISTORIS LAKE | CHOCOLATE

VISTORIS LAKE | CHERRY | CAMEO PINK

VISTORIS LAKE | VIOLET | CREAM YELLOW

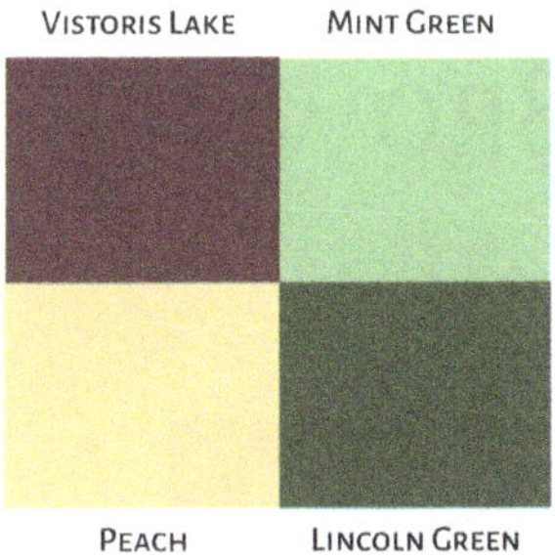
Vistoris Lake
Mint Green
Peach
Lincoln Green

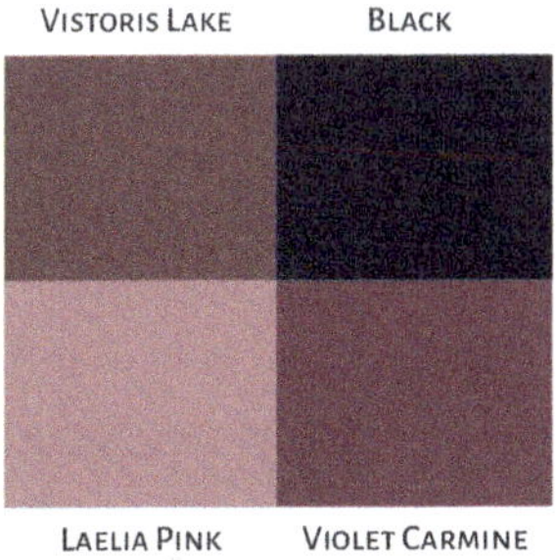
Vistoris Lake
Black
Laelia Pink
Violet Carmine

Taupe Brown

#6B3F4C

RGB : 107. 63. 76

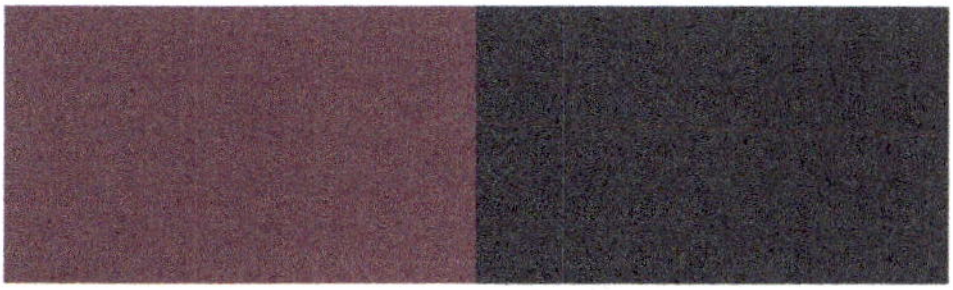

TAUPE BROWN JET BLACK

TAUPE BROWN CORAL RED ICTERINE

TAUPE BROWN ROSE QUARTZ LAVENDER

TAUPE BROWN CHERRY STEEL BLUE

Taupe Brown Pearl White

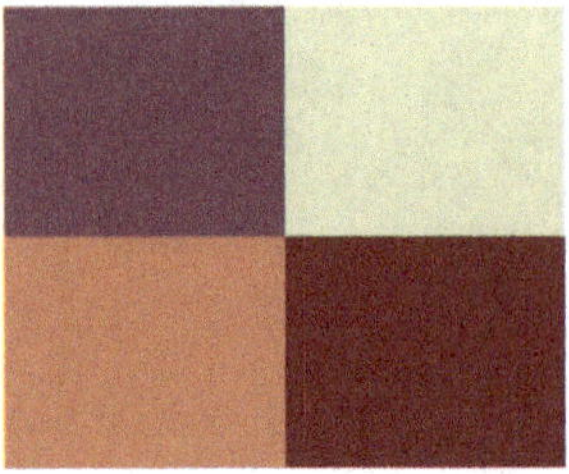

Etruscan Red Madder Brown

Taupe Brown Laelia Pink

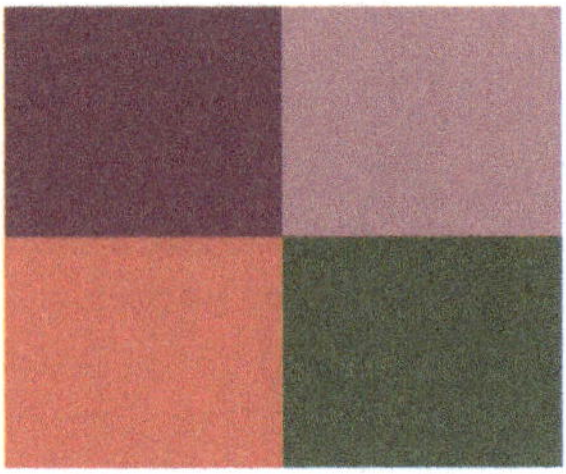

Old Red Lincoln Green

Taupe Brown Black

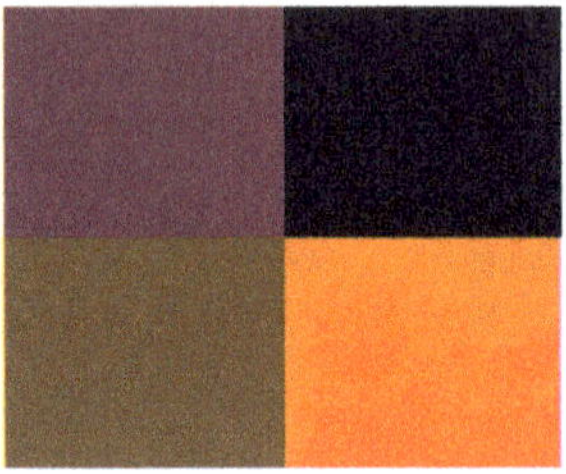

Olive Brown Pumpkin Color

Tile Color

#AB3B1E

RGB : 171. 59. 30

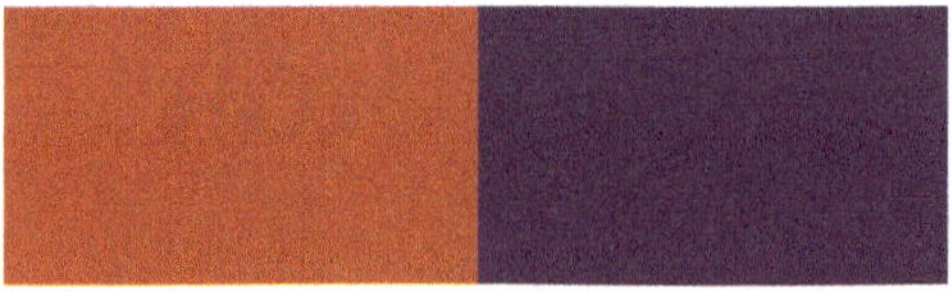

TILE COLOR AUBERGINE PURPLE

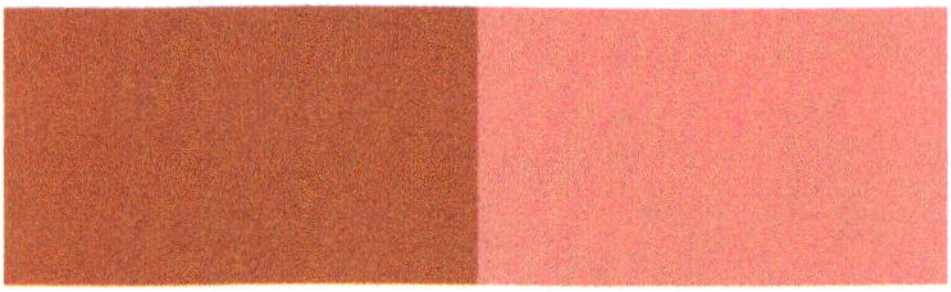

TILE COLOR EOSINE PINK

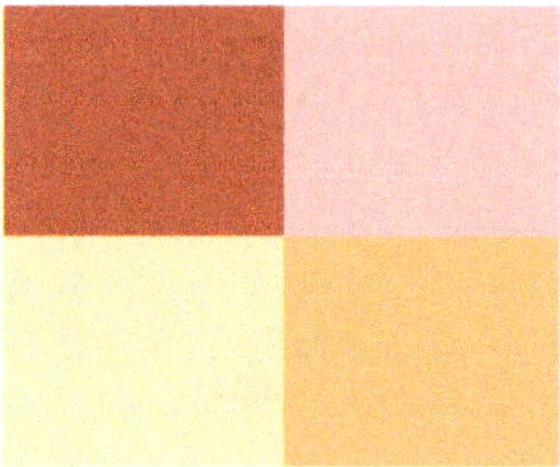
Tile Color
Rose Quartz
Beige
Cinnamon Buff

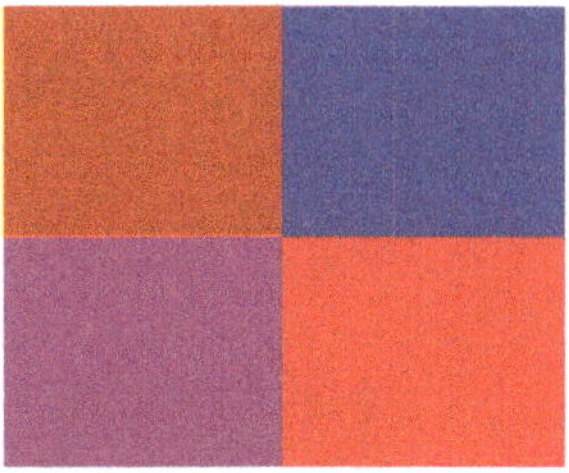
Tile Color
Blue Violet
Fandango
Rare Rhubarb

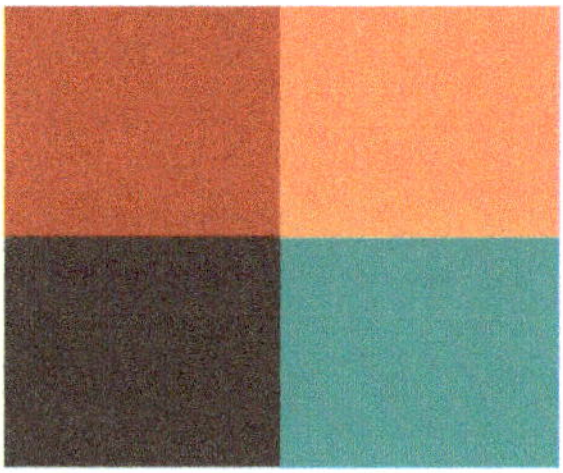
Tile Color
Pink Orange
Vandyke Brown
Dark Cyan

Corn Snake

#AB6134

RGB: 171. 97. 52

CORN SNAKE CITRON YELLOW

CORN SNAKE ANTWARP BLUE

CORN SNAKE ANTWARP BLUE

THISTLE ETON BLUE

Vermilion

#E62E00

RGB : 230. 46. 0

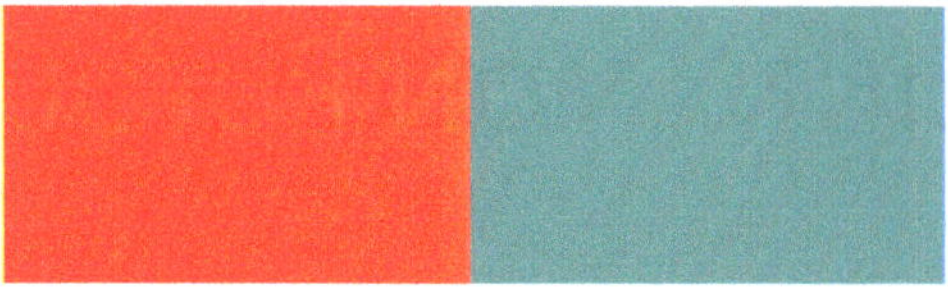

VERMILION CADET BLUE

VERMILION PEACOCK BLUE BRONZE

VERMILION BLACK IVORY

VERMILION FAWN

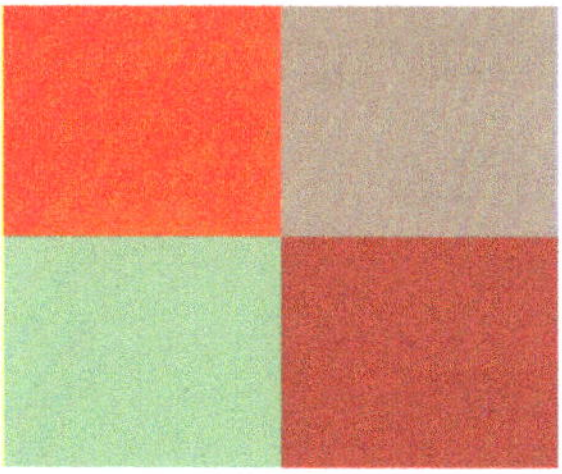

MINT GREEN UPSDELL RED

VERMILION VIOLET BLUE

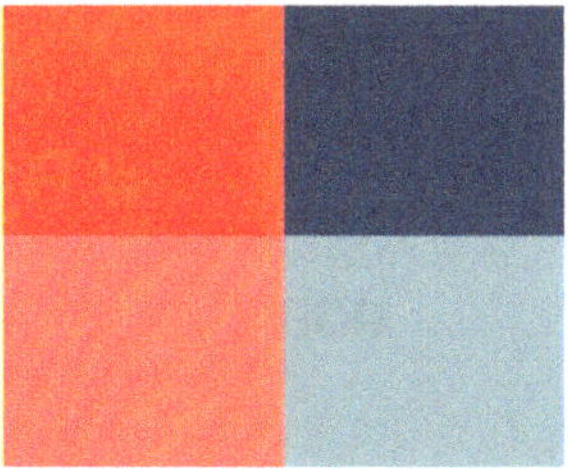

SALMON PASTEL BLUE

Cinnamon Rufous

B36E46

RGB : 179. 110. 70

Cinnamon Rufous | Grayish Lavender

Cinnamon Rufous | Dark Citrine

Cinnamon Rufous | Dusky Madder Violet

Cinnamon Rufous | Malachite | Icterine

Cinnamon Rufous | Antwarp Blue | Aubergine Purple

Cinnamon Rufous | Purple Traffic | Pastel Blue

Cinnamon Rufous | Rose Quartz | Persian Orange

Orange Citrine

#8A6632

RGB : 138. 102. 50

ORANGE CITRINE ALICE BLUE POMPEIAN RED

ORANGE CITRINE ROSE QUARTZ

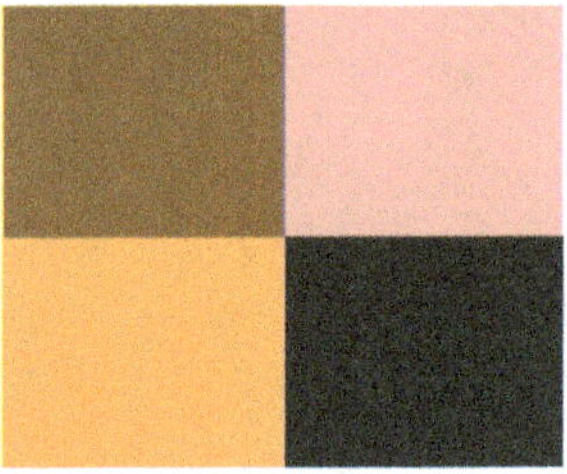

CREAM YELLOW SLATE GREEN

Isabella Color

#BD9F69

RGB : 189. 159. 105

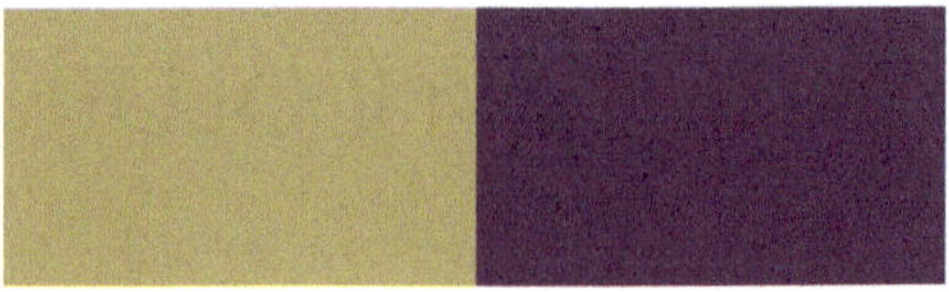

ISABELLA COLOR AUBERGINE PURPLE

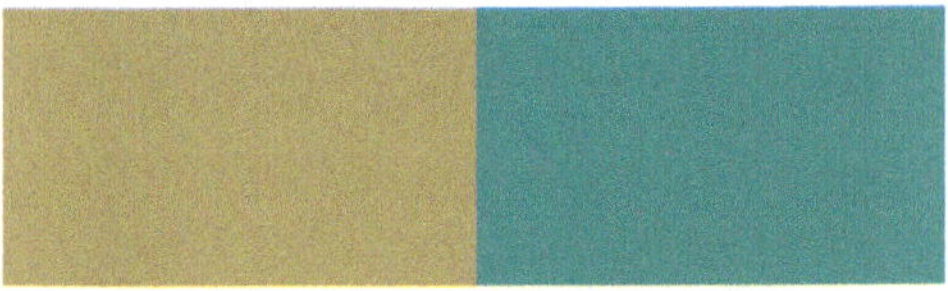

ISABELLA COLOR GREEN BLUE

ISABELLA COLOR RED ORANGE

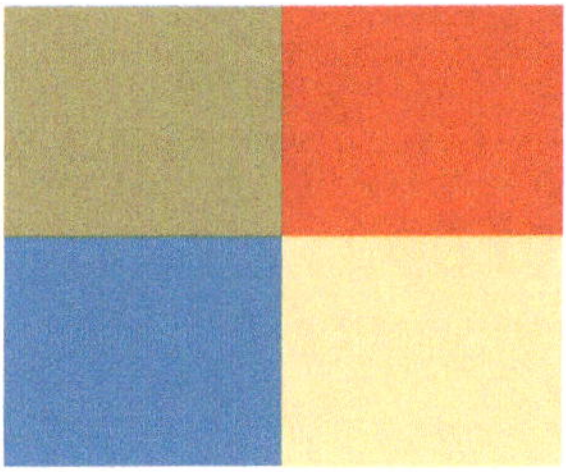

STEEL BLUE PEACH

ISABELLA COLOR PEARL WHITE

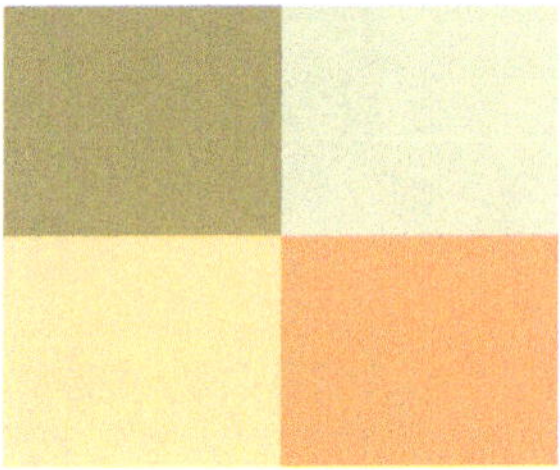

PEACH MIDDLE YELLOW RED

Fallow Color

#C19A6B

RGB : 193. 154. 107

FALLOW COLOR LILAC

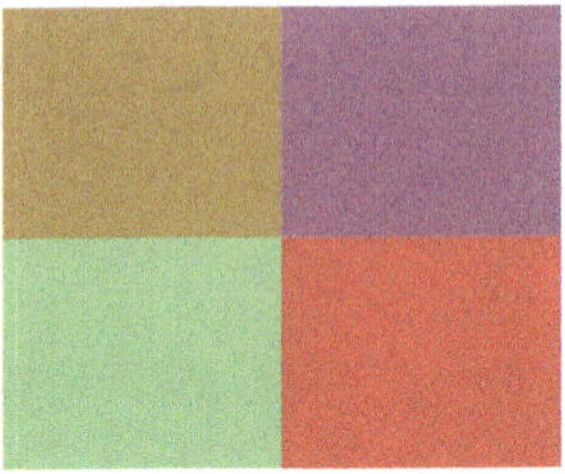

MINT GREEN OLD RED

IVORY

#F3E5AB

RGB : 243. 229. 171

IVORY SILVER

IVORY DUSKY MADDER VIOLET

IVORY BRITISH RACING GREEN

IVORY CHOCOLATE

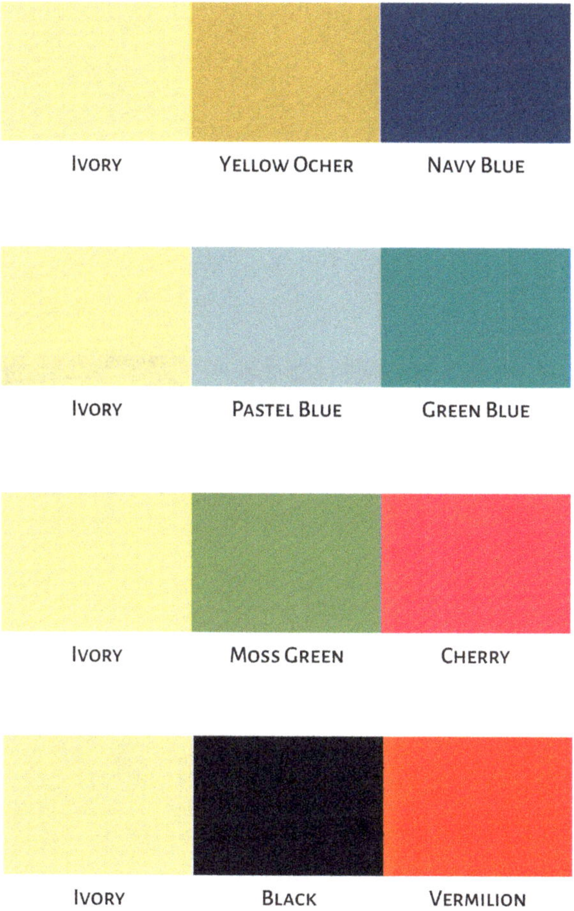
Ivory
Yellow Ocher
Navy Blue
Ivory
Pastel Blue
Green Blue
Ivory
Moss Green
Cherry
Ivory
Black
Vermilion

Ivory | Pumpkin Color | Alice Blue

Ivory | Mahogany | Violet

Ivory | Pumpkin Color | Grayish Lavender

Ivory Olive Green

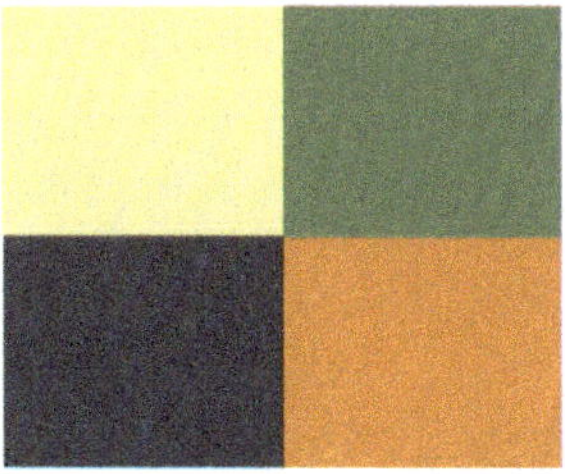

Jet Black Bronze

Ivory Chartreuse

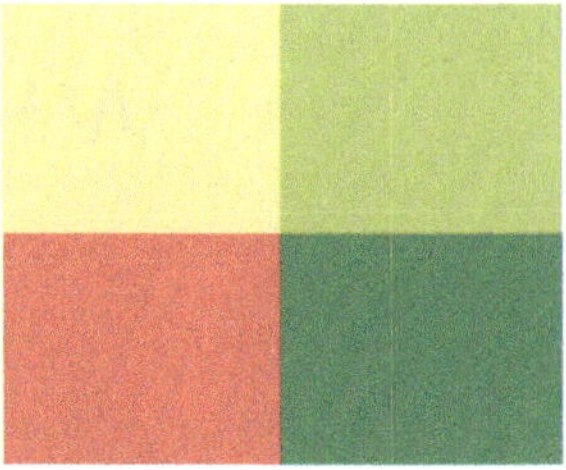

Old Red Cossack Green

Ivory Rare Rhubarb

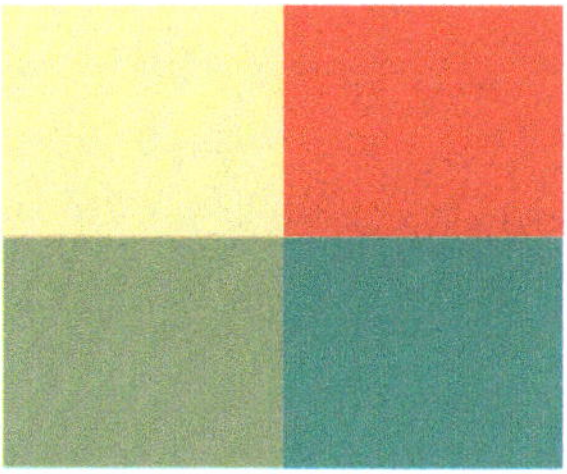

Rainette Green Pine Green

Ivory Rainette Green

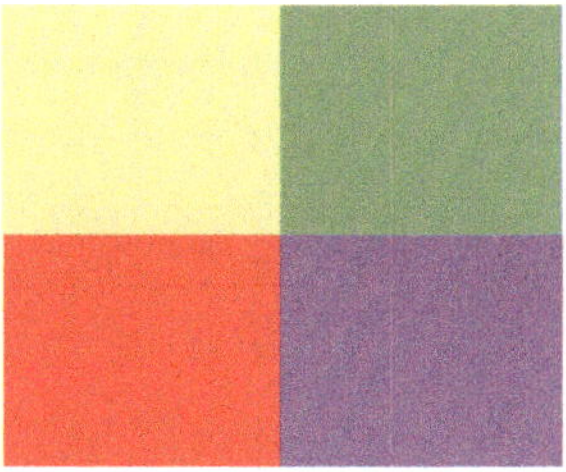

Rare Rhubarb Aconite Violet

Ivory Sienna

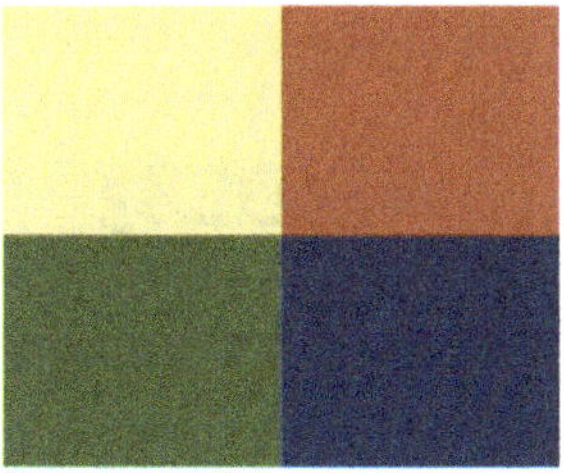

Army Green Duke Blue

Wheat

#F5DEB3

RGB : 245. 222. 179

Wheat Pearl White

Icterine Turquoise Green

Pumpkin Color

#FF8000

RGB : 255. 128. 0

Pumpkin Color Dark Blue

Pumpkin Color Dusky Madder Violet

Pumpkin Color Violet Blue

Pumpkin Color Duke Blue Beige

Pumpkin Color | Glaucous Green | Pale Burnt Lake

Pumpkin Color | Alice Blue | Ivory

Pumpkin Color | Yellow Ocher | Chocolate

Pumpkin Color | Ivory | Lavender

PUMPKIN COLOR BLUE

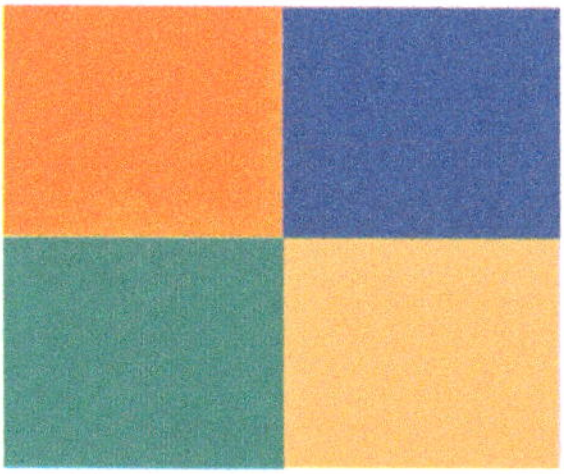

PINE GREEN CREAM YELLOW

PUMPKIN COLOR OLIVE BROWN

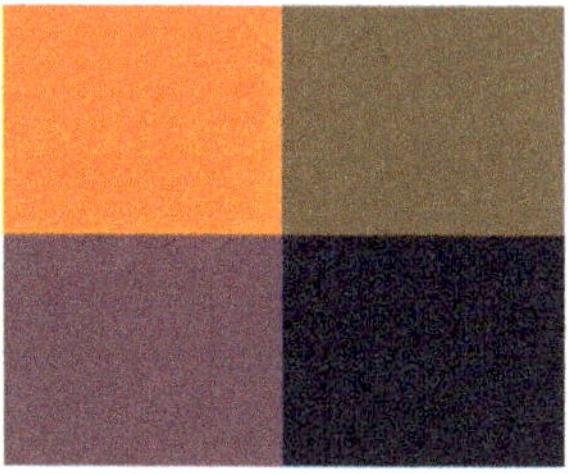

TAUPE BROWN BLACK

PUMPKIN COLOR SIENNA

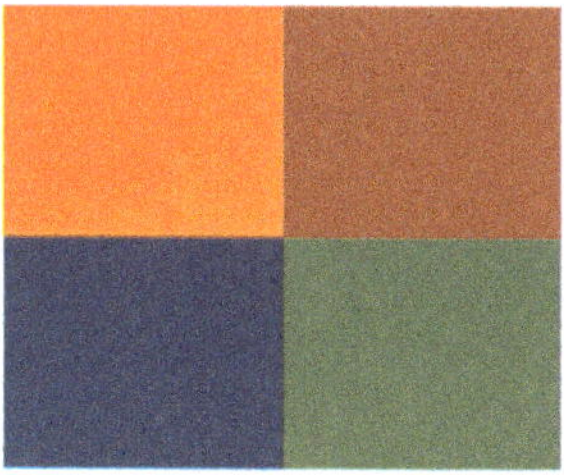

VIOLET BLUE OLIVE GREEN

PUMPKIN COLOR SIENNA

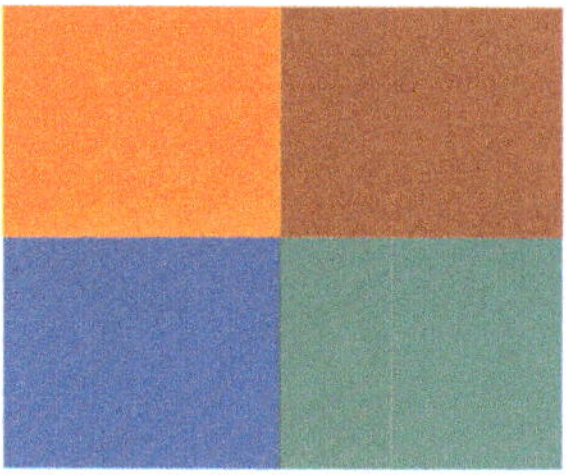

ROYAL BLUE WINTERGREEN DREAM

PUMPKIN COLOR BRONZE

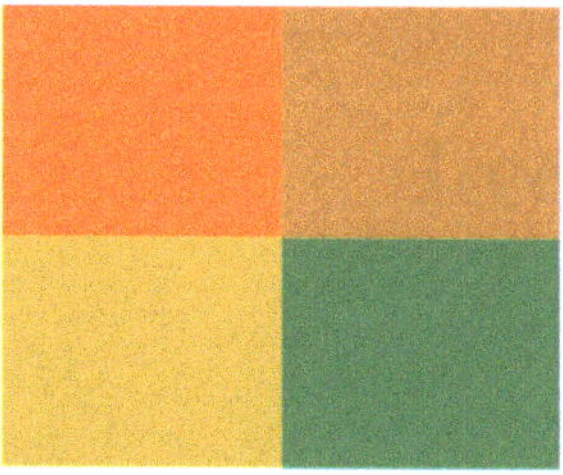

MUSTARD YELLOW COSSACK GREEN

PUMPKIN COLOR VIOLET

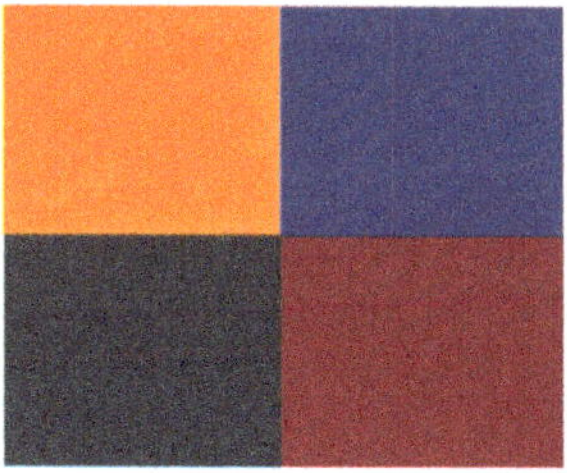

JET BLACK BURGUNDY

CHOCOLATE

#D2691E

RGB : 210. 105. 30

Chocolate Victoris Lake

Chocolate Ivory

Chocolate Lima

Chocolate Pumpkin Color Yellow Ocher

Light Naples Yellow

#FFF6AD

RGB : 255. 246. 173

LIGHT NAPLES YELLOW CHERRY

LIGHT NAPLES YELLOW ALMAGRE

LIGHT NAPLES YELLOW GRENADINE PINK DARK GREEN CYAN

LIGHT NAPLES YELLOW GRENADINE PINK DARK CYAN

Light Naples Yellow — Almagre

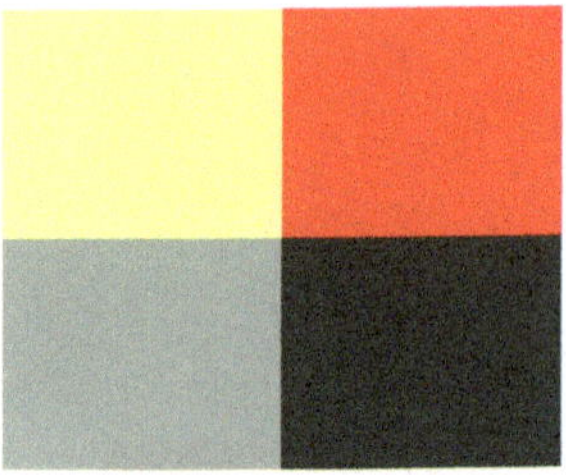

Neutral Gray — Slate Green

Light Naples Yellow — Old Red

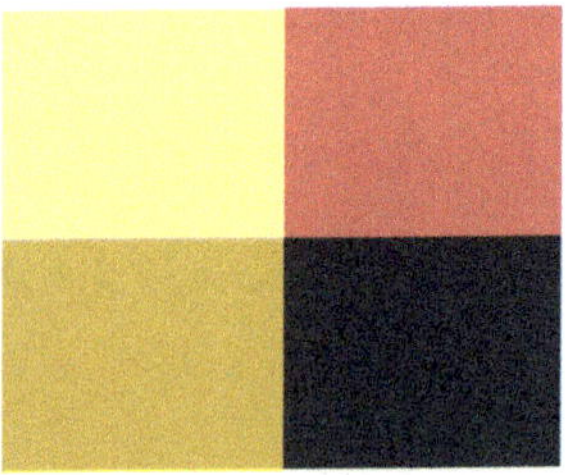

Yellow Ocher — Dark Green Cyan

Mustard Yellow

#E1AD01

RGB : 225. 173. 1

Mustard Yellow | Moss Green

Mustard Yellow | Khaki | Alice Blue

Mustard Yellow | Turquoise Green | Antwarp Blue

Mustard Yellow | Green | Sienna

Mustard Yellow

Aquamarine

Vinaceous Cinnamon

Mustard Yellow

Bronze

Pine Green

Navy Blue

Mustard Yellow

Olive Yellow

Magenta Pink

Might Night Blue

Mustard Yellow

Crimson Color

Sea Green

British Racing Green

Mustard Yellow

Citron Yellow

Turquoise Green

Middle Yellow Red

Pyrite Yellow

#C0AC56

RGB : 192. 172. 86

PYRITE YELLOW THISTLE GLAUCOUS GREEN

PYRITE YELLOW ALMAGRE

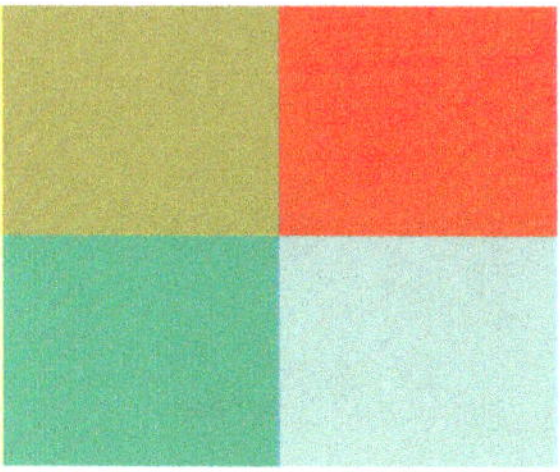

SEA GREEN NILE BLUE

PYRITE YELLOW BLACK

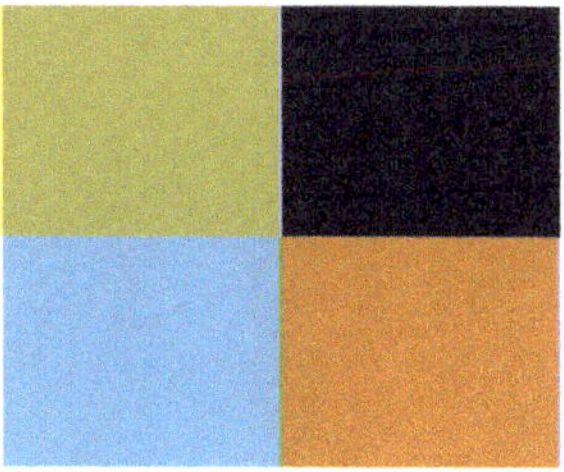

LIGHT BLUE BRONZE

PYRITE YELLOW LIGHT BLUE

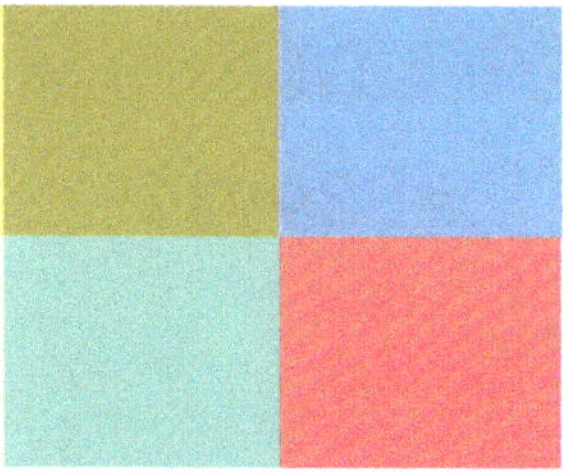

AQUAMARINE EOSINE PINK

SULPHINE YELLOW

#B89932

RGB: 184. 153. 50

Sulphine Yellow | Turquoise Green

Sulphine Yellow | Light Blue

Sulphine Yellow | Hydrangea Red | Alice Blue

Sulphine Yellow | Coffee | Steel Blue

SULPHINE YELLOW OLD RED

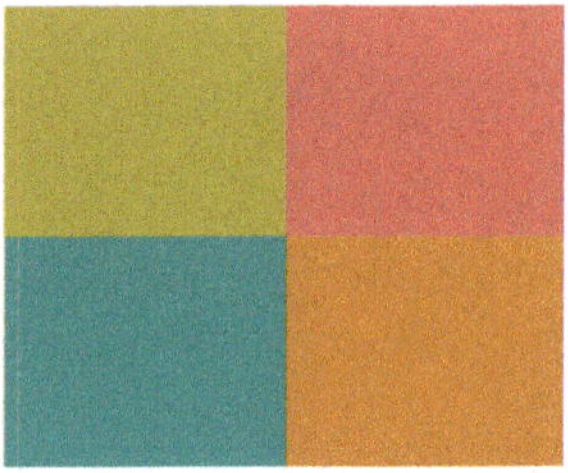

GREEN BLUE BRONZE

OLIVE OCHER

#CCAD44

RGB : 204. 173. 68

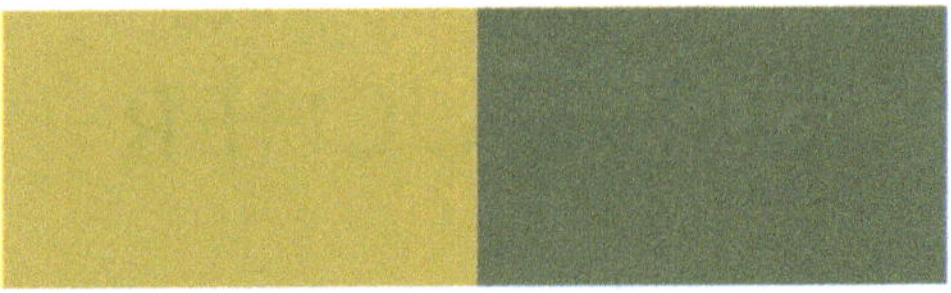

Olive Ocher Olive Green

Olive Ocher Gold Cadet Blue

Olive Ocher Orange Dark Green Cyan

Olive Ocher Violet Mint Green

Olive Ocher | Pansy Purple | Indigo Blue

Olive Ocher | Pearl White

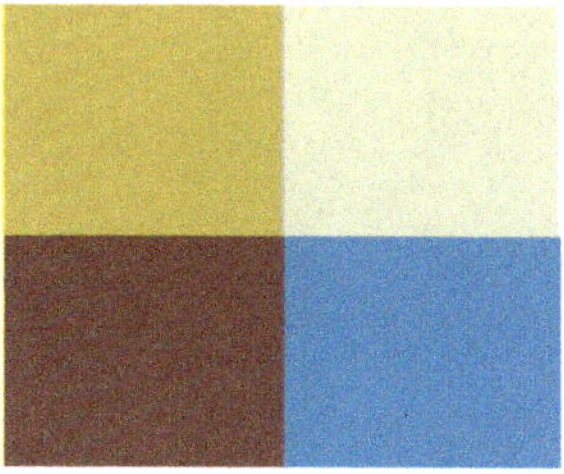

Cuttlefish | Steel Blue

Olive Ocher | British Racing Green

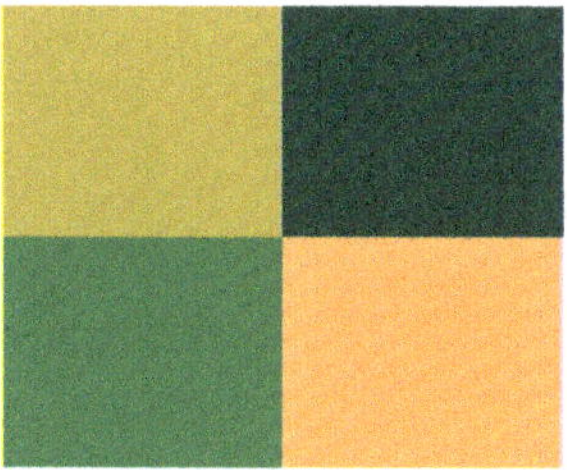

Cossack Green | Cream Yellow

Light Green Yellow

#BFCC54

RGB : 191. 204. 84

Light Green Yellow — Cotinga Purple

Light Green Yellow — Violet Blue

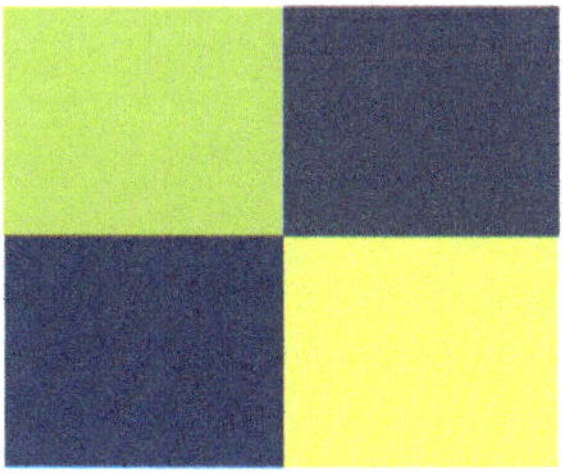

Might Night Blue — Icterine

Light Green Yellow — Sea Green

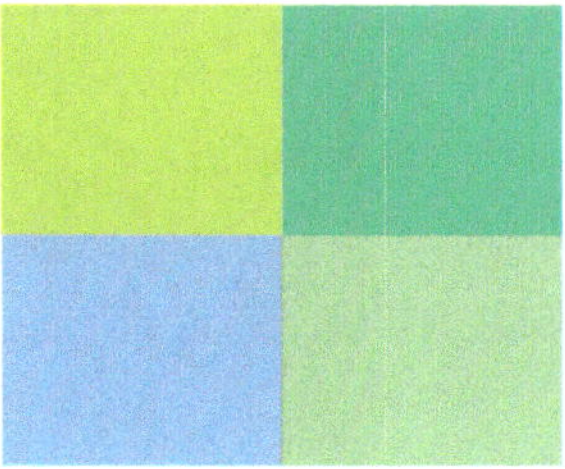

Light Blue — Mint Green

Light Green Yellow — Cream Yellow

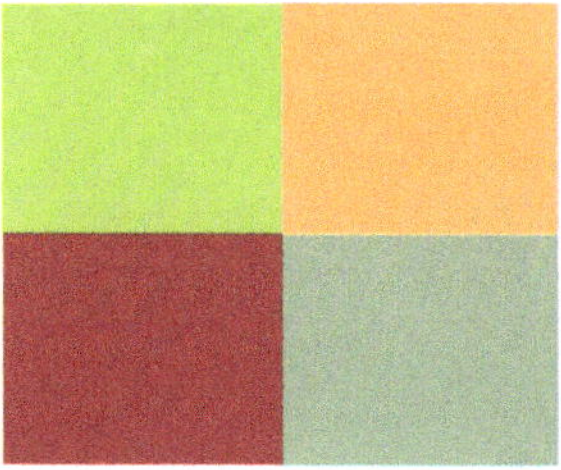

Pompeian Red — Laurel Green

Light Green Yellow — Eton Blue

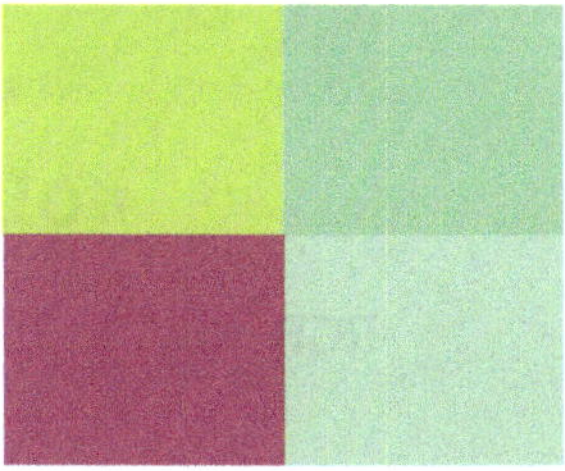

Purple Traffic — Turquoise Green

Malachite

#0BDA51

RGB : 11. 218. 81

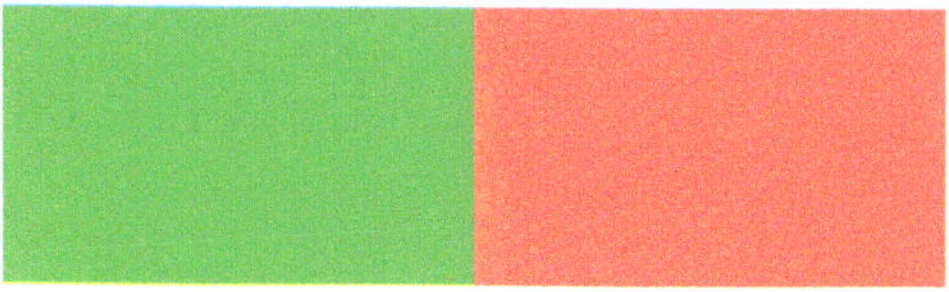

MALACHITE SALMON

MALACHITE ICTERINE CINNAMON RUFOUS

MALACHITE ALMAGRE

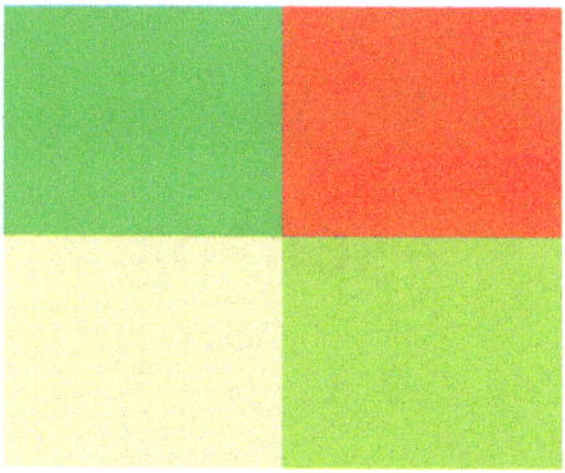

BEIGE PALE GREEN

Avocado Green

#568203

RGB : 86. 130. 3

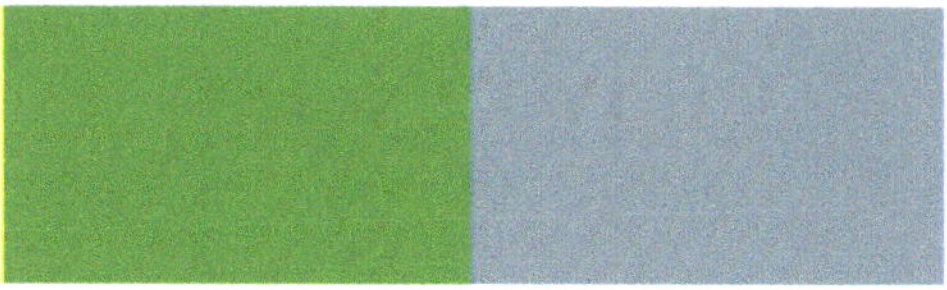

Avocado Green Alice Blue

Avocado Green Cherry White

Olive Buff

#BCC08E

RGB : 188. 192. 142

Olive Buff　Violet Blue

Olive Buff　Middle Yellow Red　Blue Violet

Olive Buff　Royal Red　Jade

Olive Buff　Nile Blue

Alice Blue　Green Blue

Olive Buff　Cotinga Purple

Cossack Green　Slate Green

Buffy Citrine

#8B7F4B

RGB : 139. 127. 75

BUFFY CITRINE SAPPHIRE

BUFFY CITRINE PALE BURNT LAKE GRAYISH LAVENDER

BUFFY CITRINE VIOLET BLUE ROYAL RED

Dark Citrine

#827B54

RGB : 130. 123. 84

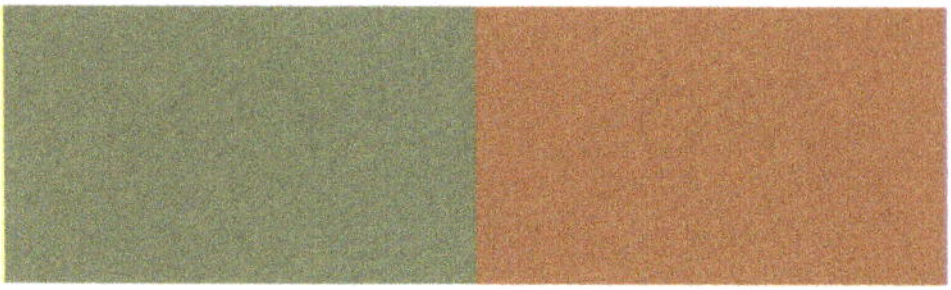

DARK CITRINE CINNAMON RUFOUS

DARK CITRINE LIGHT BLUE

DARK CITRINE ALMAGRE

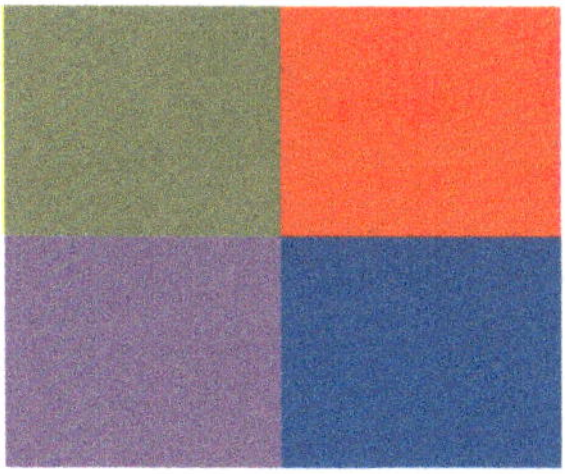

LIGHT MAUVE INDIGO BLUE

DARK CITRINE PINE GREEN

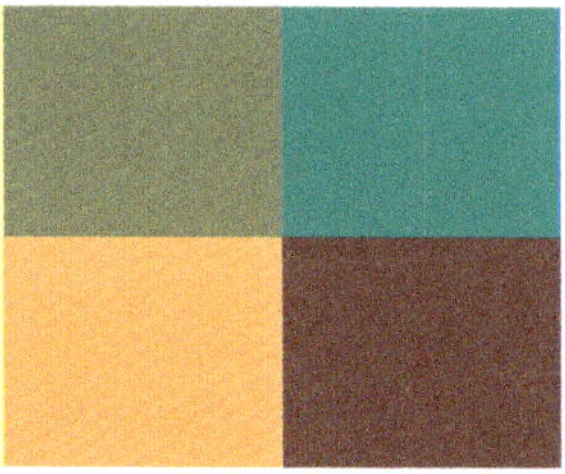

CREAM YELLOW CUTTLEFISH

Moss Green

#8A9A5B

RGB : 138. 154. 91

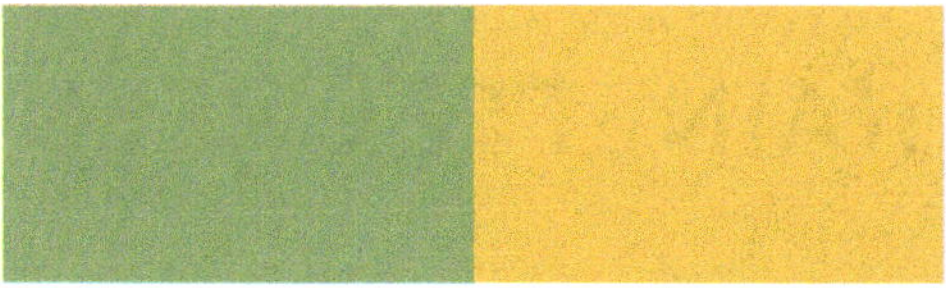

MOSS GREEN MUSTARD YELLOW

MOSS GREEN IVORY CHERRY

Rainette Green

#8899CB

RGB : 136.153. 107

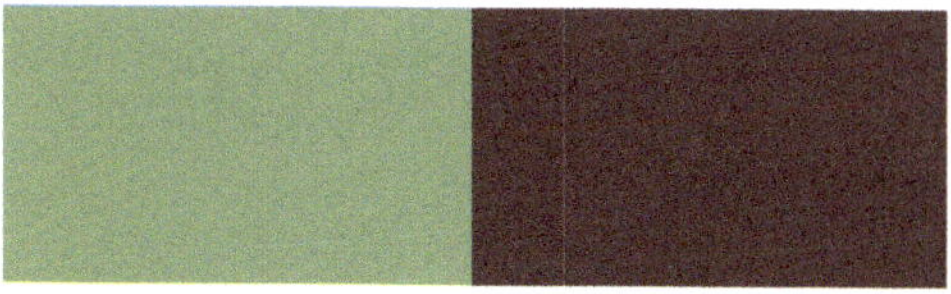

Rainette Green Coffee

Rainette Green Magenta Pink Lilac

Rainette Green Mint Green Alice Blue

Rainette Green Ivory

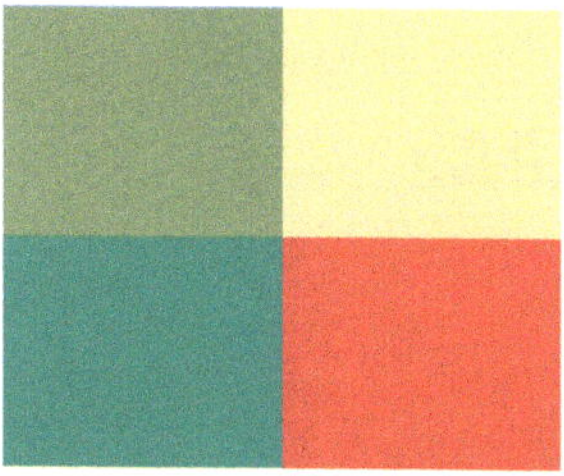

Pine Green Rare Rhubarb

Rainette Green Ivory

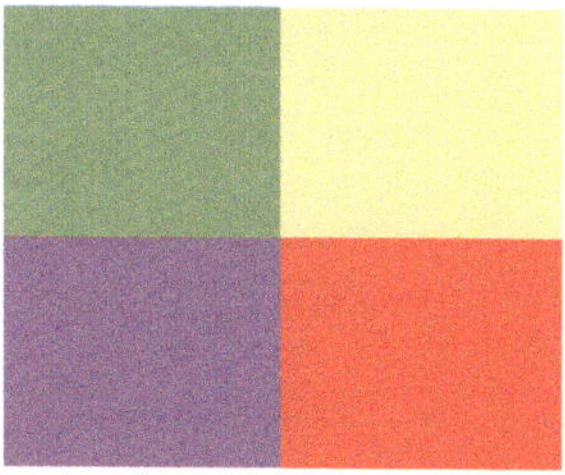

Aconite Violet Rare Rhubarb

Eton Blue

#96C8A2

RGB : 150. 200 162

Eton Blue Antwarp Blue

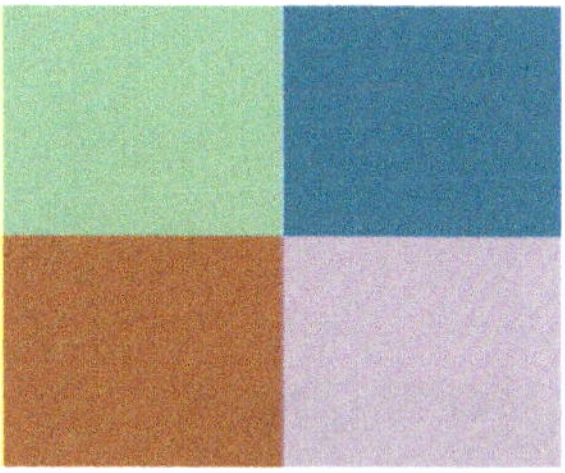

Corn Snake Thistle

Eton Blue Purple Traffic

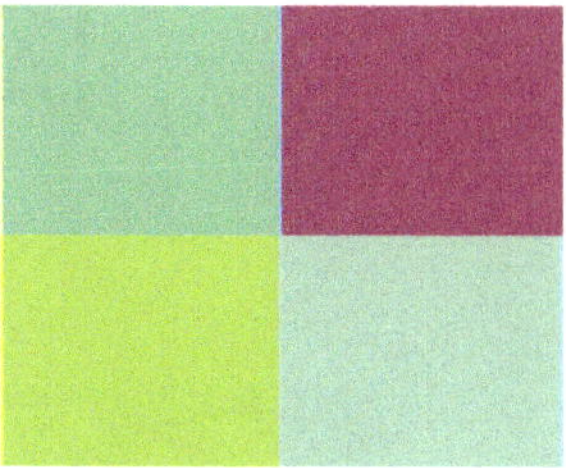

Light Green Yellow Turquoise Green

Jade

#00A86B

RGB : 0. 168. 107

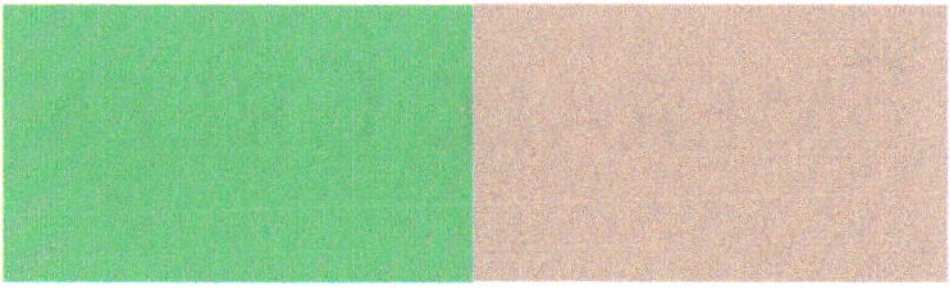

Jade Cameo Pink

Jade Olive Buff Royal Red

Jade Tomato British Racing Green

Jade Amaranth

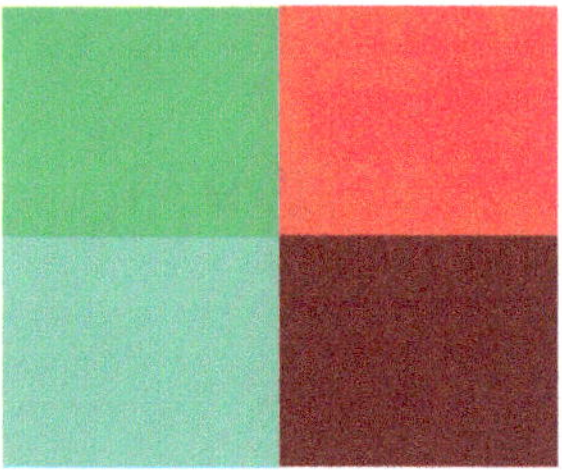

Venice Green Pale Burnt Lake

Emerald Green

#009975

RGB : 0. 153. 117

EMERALD GREEN UPSDELL RED AUBERGINE PURPLE

EMERALD GREEN ORANGE

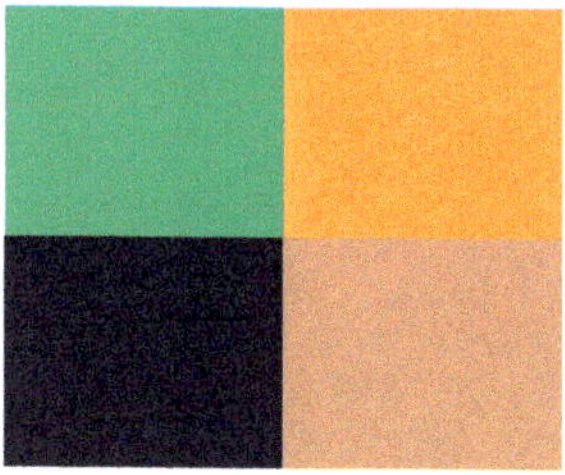

BLACK VINACEOUS CINNAMON

EMERALD GREEN ICTERINE

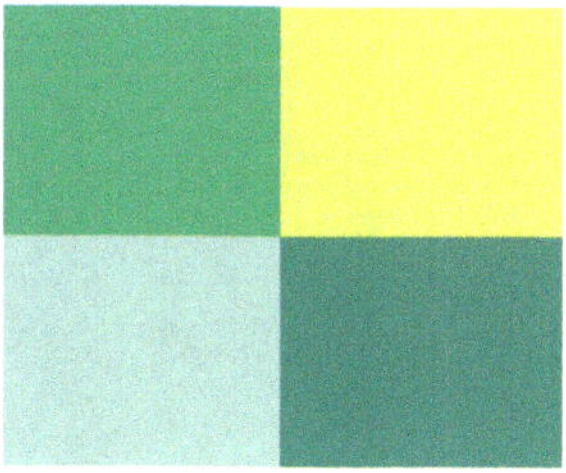

NILE BLUE PINE GREEN

EMERALD GREEN VIOLET

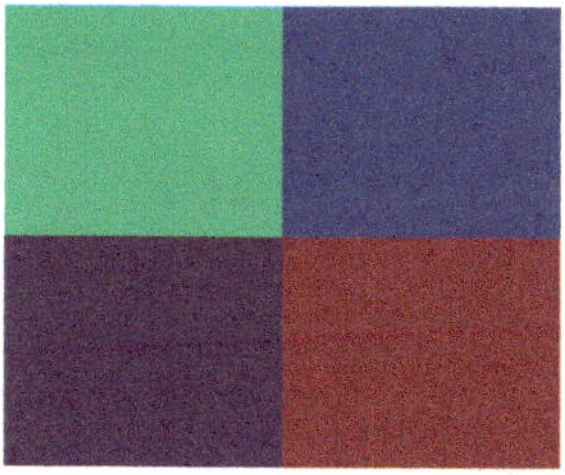

AUBERGINE PURPLE BURGUNDY

Pine Green

#01766F

RGB : 1.121.111

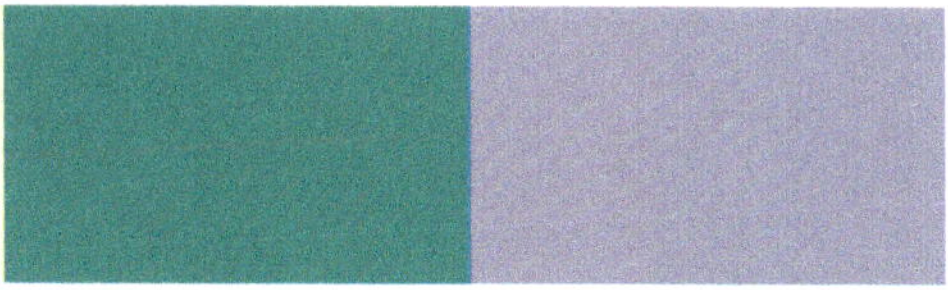

PINE GREEN GRAYISH LAVENDER

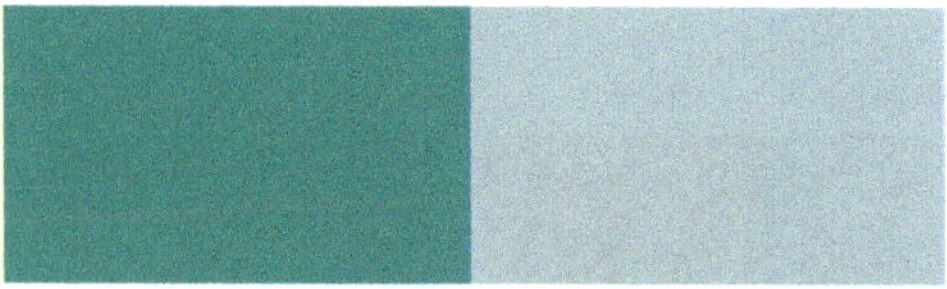

PINE GREEN PASTEL BLUE

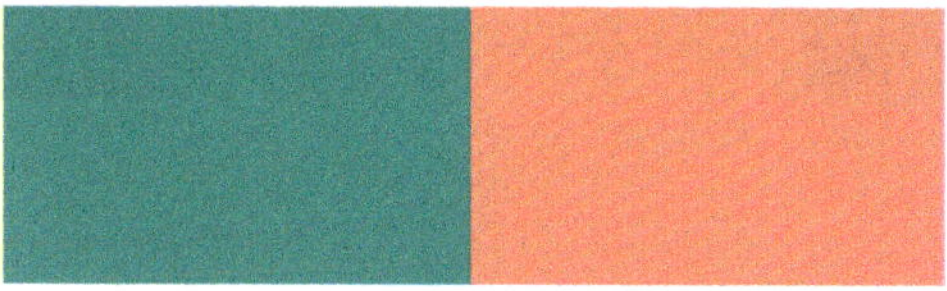

PINE GREEN CORAL RED

PINE GREEN RASPBERRY RED CREAM YELLOW

PINE GREEN TOMATO DEEP INDIGO

PINE GREEN BRONZE

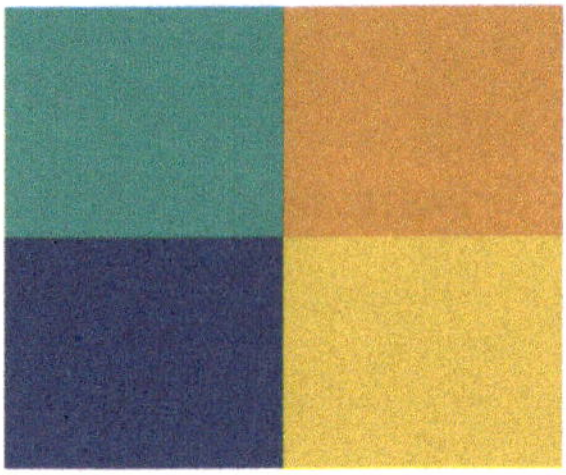

NAVY BLUE MUSTARD YELLOW

PINE GREEN IVORY

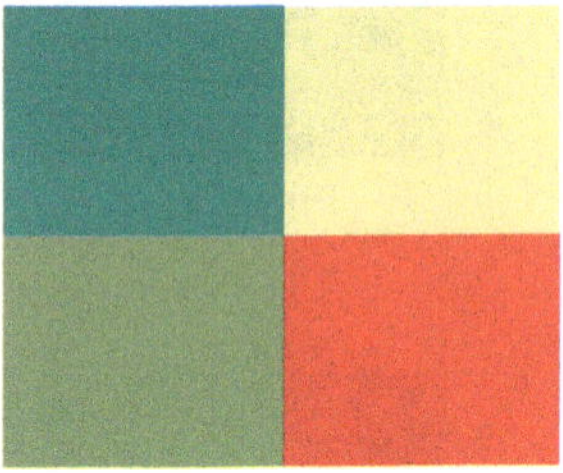

RAINETTE GREEN RARE RHUBARB

PINE GREEN BLUE

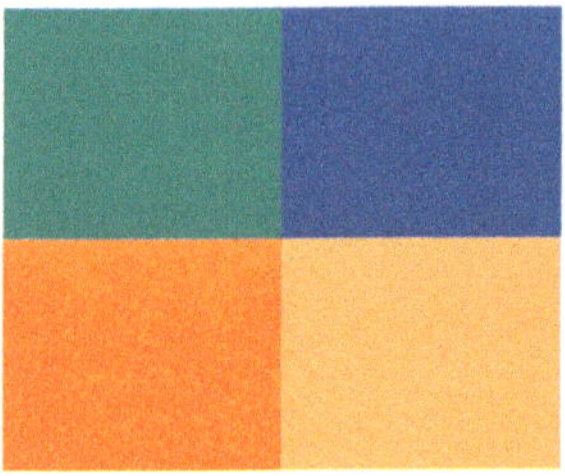

PUMPKIN COLOR CREAM YELLOW

PINE GREEN MINT GREEN

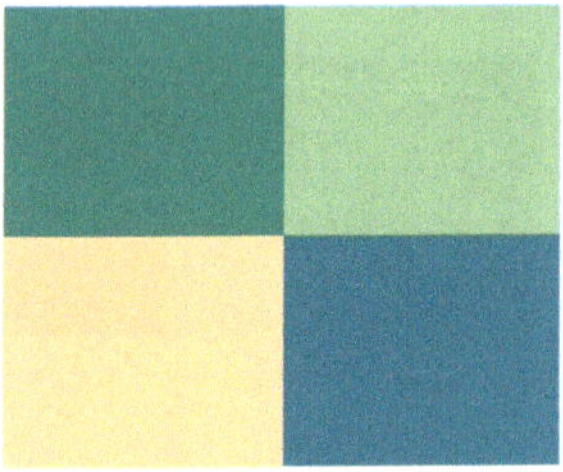

PEACH ANTWARP BLUE

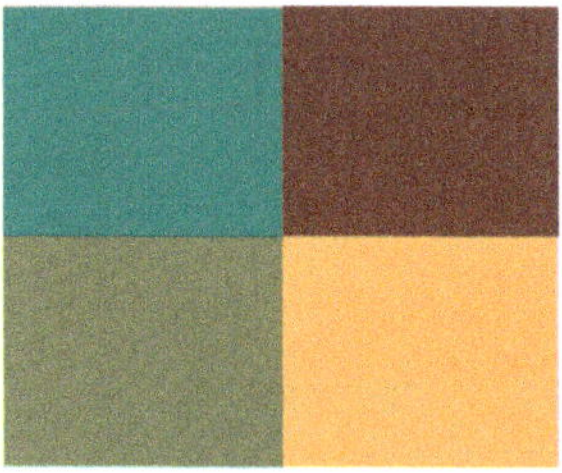
Pine Green
Cuttlefish
Dark Citrine
Cream Yellow

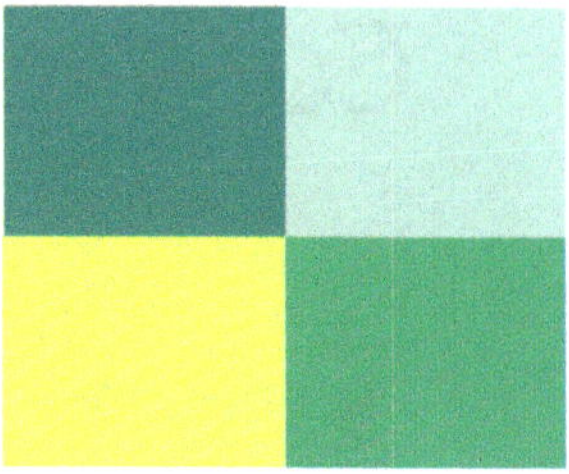
Pine Green
Nile Blue
Icterine
Emerald Green

Cossack Green

#416F3F

RGB : 65. 111.63

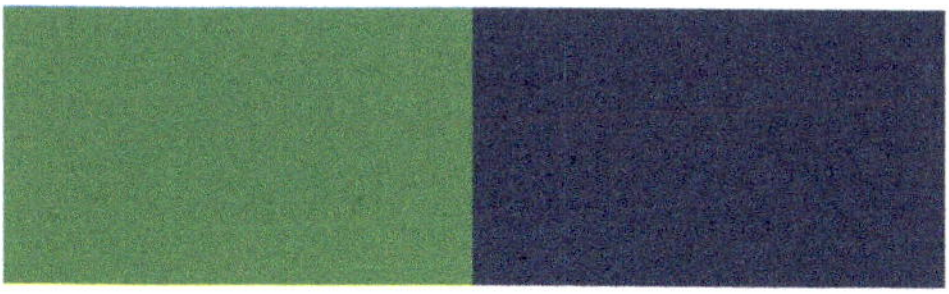

COSSACK GREEN | DUKE BLUE

COSSACK GREEN | ALICE BLUE | BEIGE

Cossack Green | Chartreuse

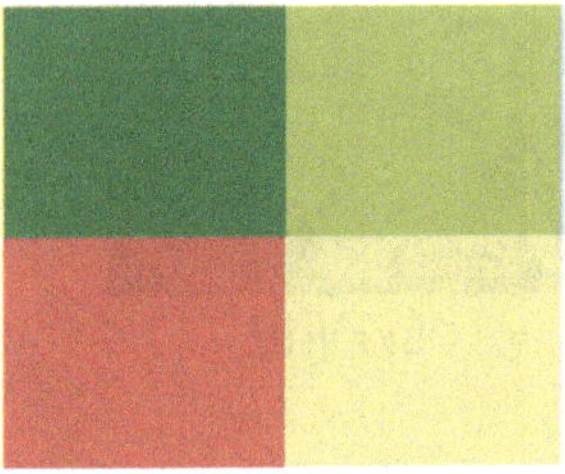

Old Red | Ivory

Cossack Green | Old Red

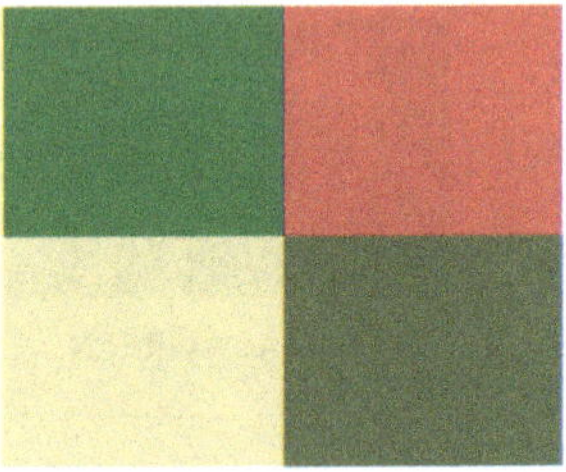

Beige | Olive Green

Cossack Green | British Racing Green

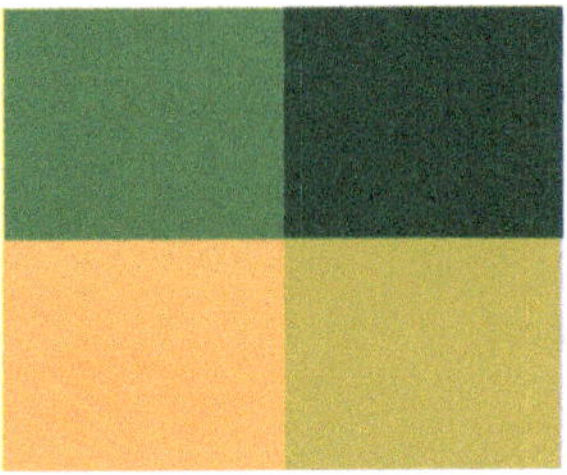

Cream Yellow | Olive Ocher

Cossack Green | Beige

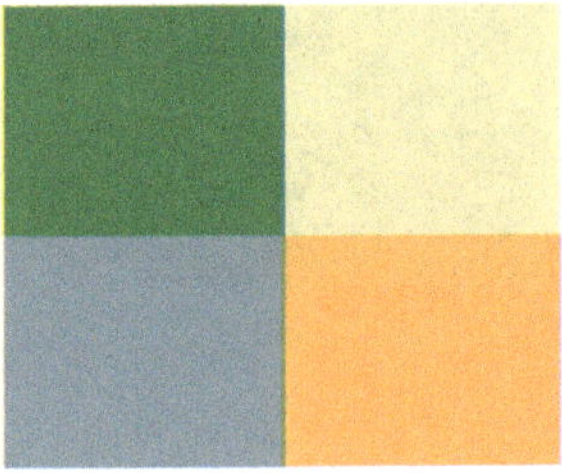

Alice Blue | Cream Yellow

Cossack Green | Bronze

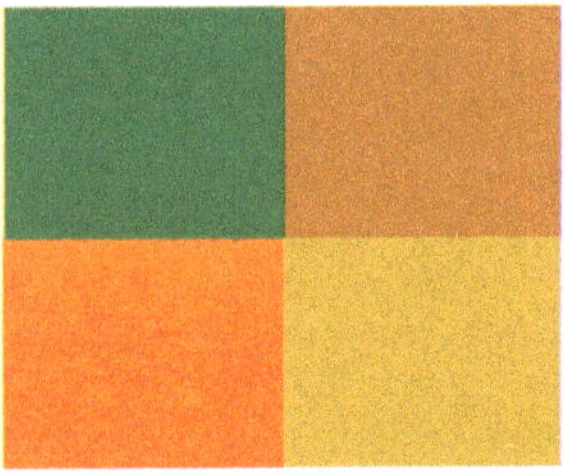

Pumpkin Color | Mustard Yellow

Cossack Green | Grenadine Pink

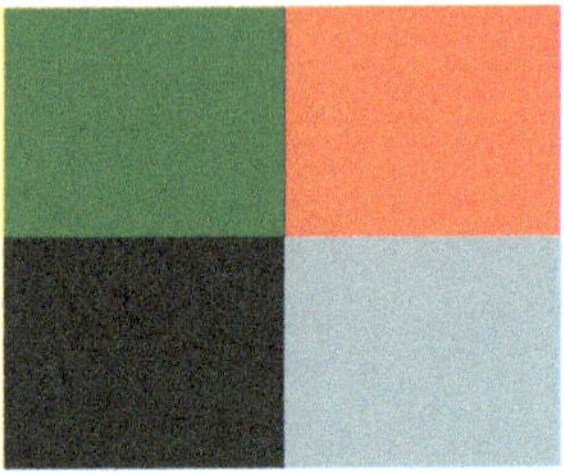

Slate Green | Pastel Blue

British Racing Green

#004225

RGB: 0. 66. 37

British Racing Green — Ivory

British Racing Green — Tomato — Jade

British Racing Green — Raspberry Red — Dark Slate Purple

British Racing Green | Olive Ocher

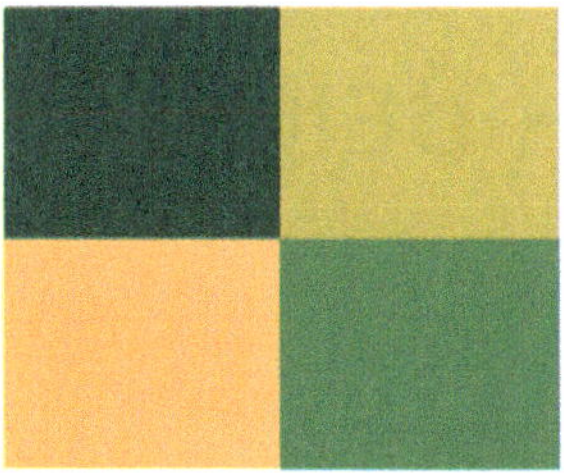

Cream Yellow | Cossack Green

British Racing Green | Sea Green

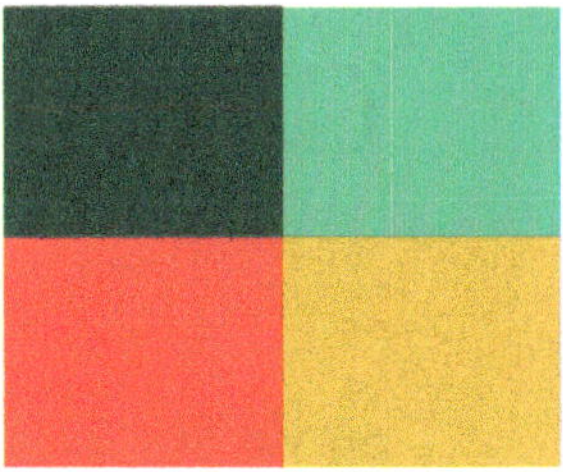

Crimson Color | Mustard Yellow

British Racing Green | Bottle Green

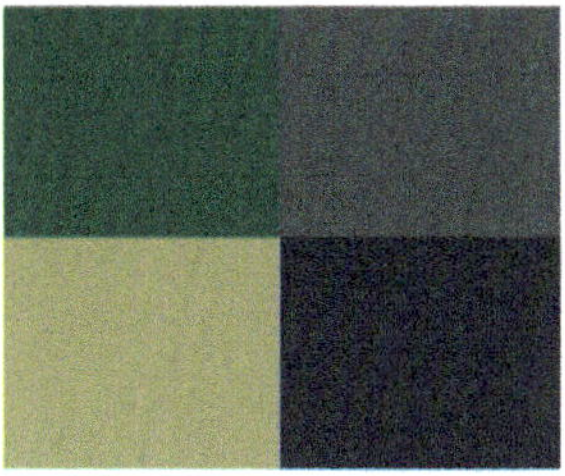

Greyish Beige | Dark Green Cyan

British Racing Green | Upsdell Red

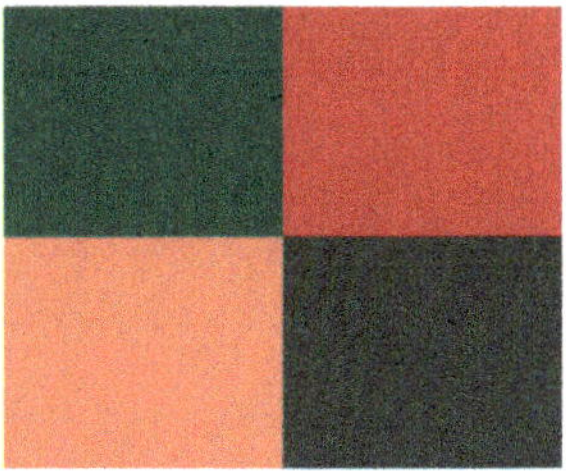

Coral Red | Slate Green

British Racing Green | Royal Red

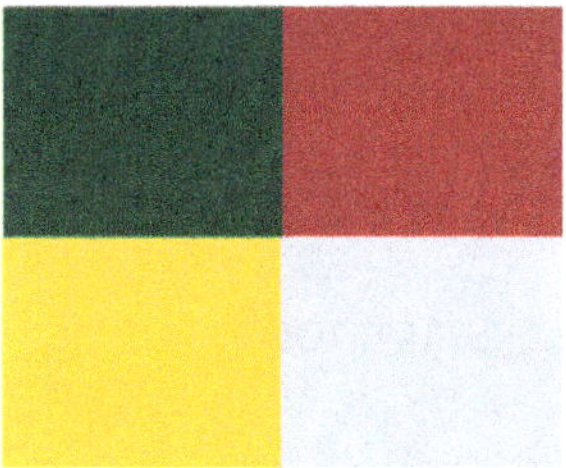

Gold | Lavender

Greyish Beige

#9E9764

RGB : 158. 151. 100

GREYISH BEIGE NAVY BLUE AMARANTH

GREYISH BEIGE BOTTLE GREEN

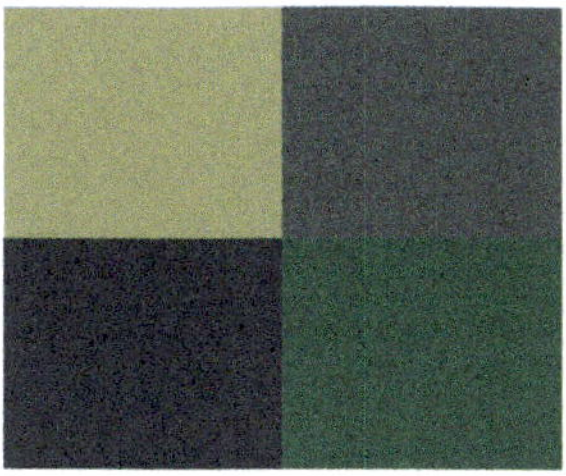

DARK GREEN CYAN BRITISH RACING GREEN

Army Green

#4B5320

RGB : 75. 83. 32

ARMY GREEN KHAKI DIAMINE GREEN

ARMY GREEN IVORY

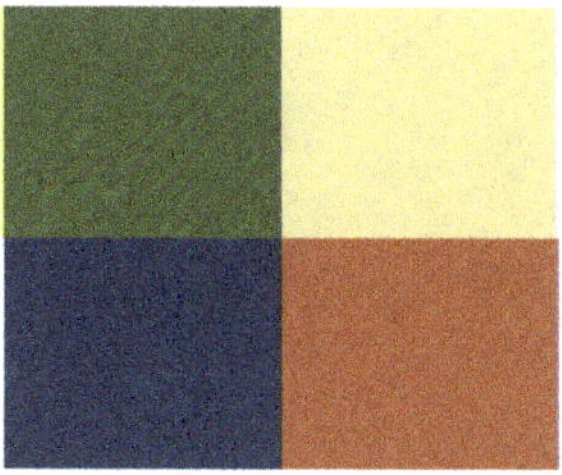

DUKE BLUE SIENNA

COFFEE

#3F2212

RGB : 63. 34. 18

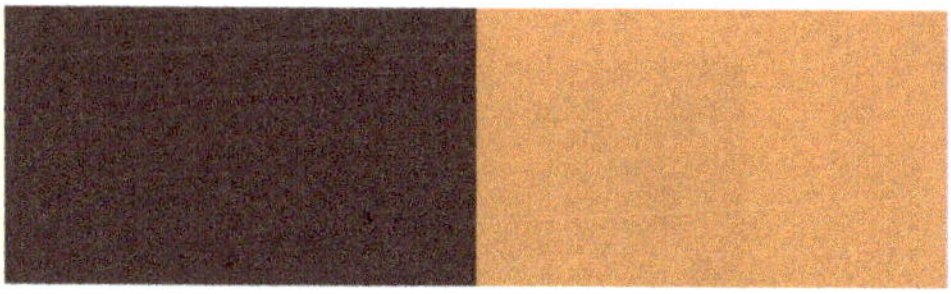

COFFEE PERSIAN ORANGE

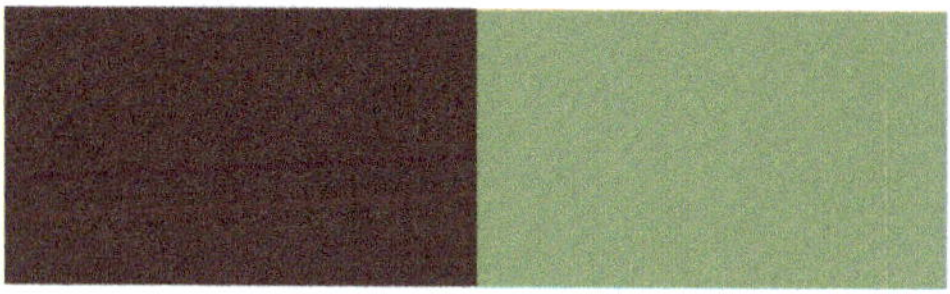

COFFEE RAINETTE GREEN

COFFEE STEEL BLUE SULPHINE YELLOW

COFFEE AQUAMARINE CINNAMON BUFF

Coffee Salmon

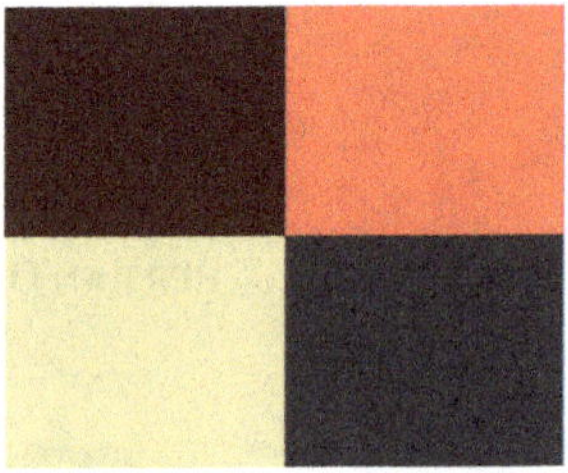

Beige Jet Black

Slate Green

#2B3423

RGB : 43. 52. 35

Slate Green | Icterine | Venice Green

Slate Green | Neutral Gray | Persian Orange

Slate Green | Nile Blue

Thistle | Bronze

Slate Green | Neutral Gray

Almagre | Light Naples Yellow

SLATE GREEN ALICE BLUE

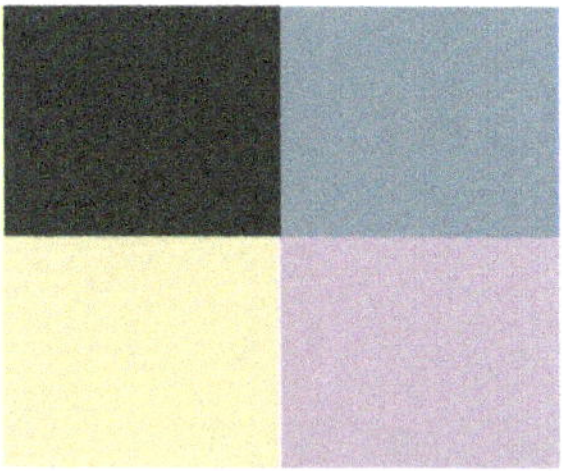

BEIGE THISTLE

SLATE GREEN UPSDELL RED

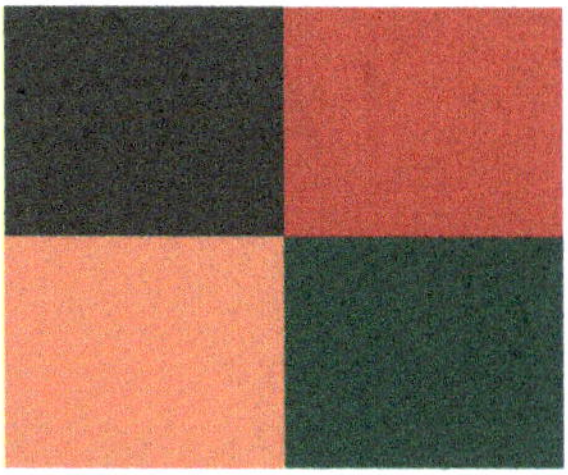

CORAL RED BRITISH RACING GREEN

SLATE GREEN COSSACK GREEN

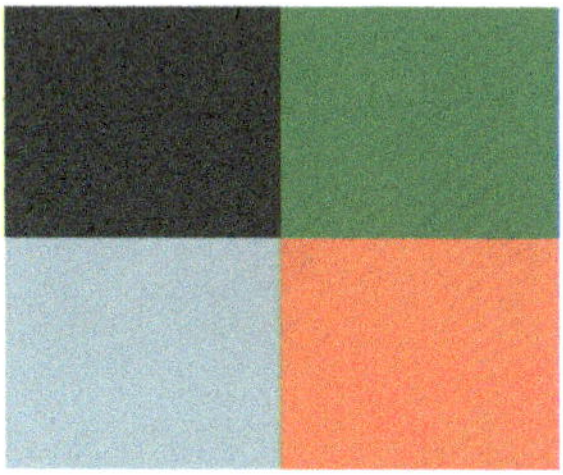

PASTEL BLUE GRENADINE PINK

SLATE GREEN CREAM YELLOW

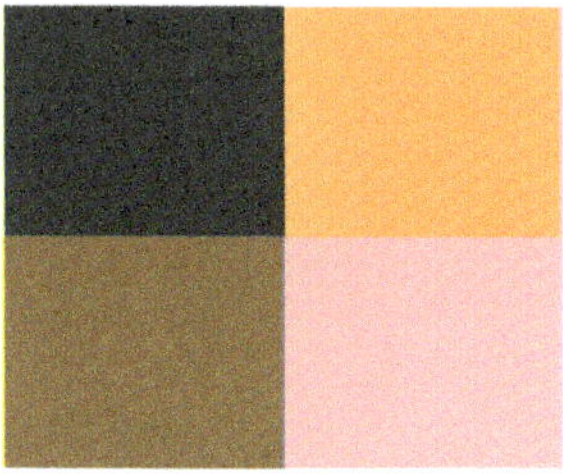

ORANGE CITRINE ROSE QUARTZ

SLATE GREEN OLIVE BUFF

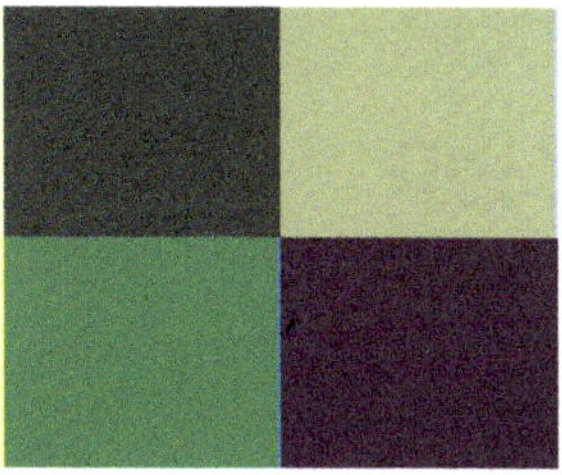

COSSACK GREEN COTINGA PURPLE

SLATE GREEN MIDDLE YELLOW RED

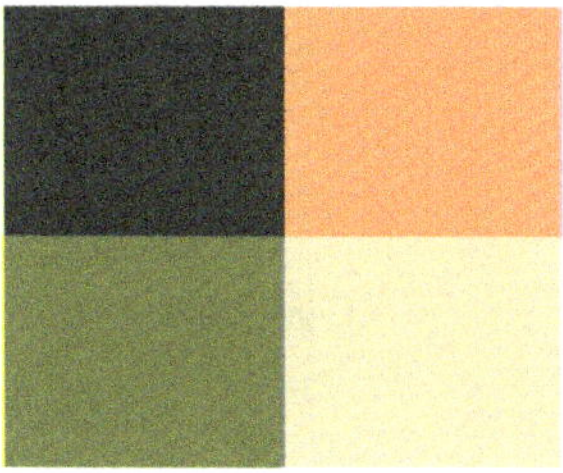

OLIVE BEIGE

LAUREL GREEN

#A9B49D

RGB : 169. 186. 157

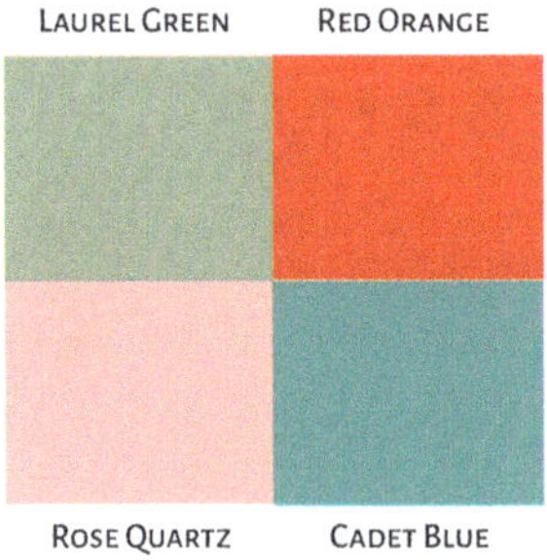
Laurel Green
Red Orange
Rose Quartz
Cadet Blue

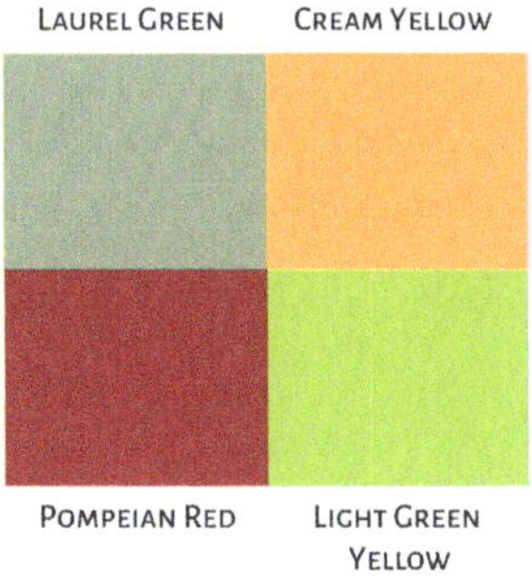
Laurel Green
Cream Yellow
Pompeian Red
Light Green Yellow

Aquamarine

#9FD5D1

RGB : 159. 213. 209

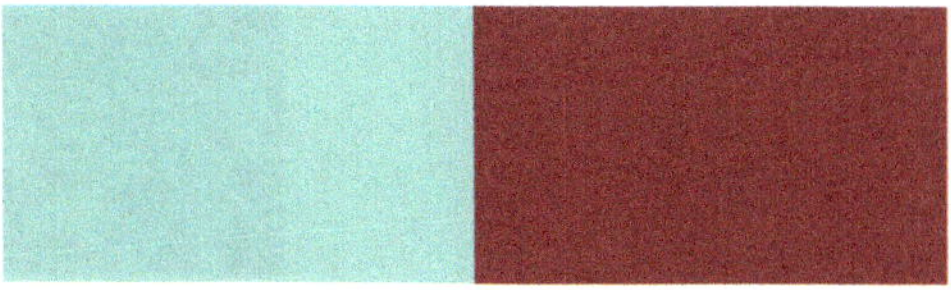

AQUAMARINE BURGUNDY

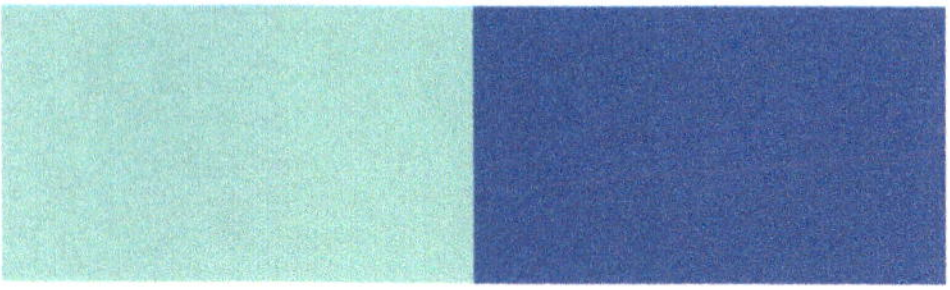

AQUAMARINE BLUE

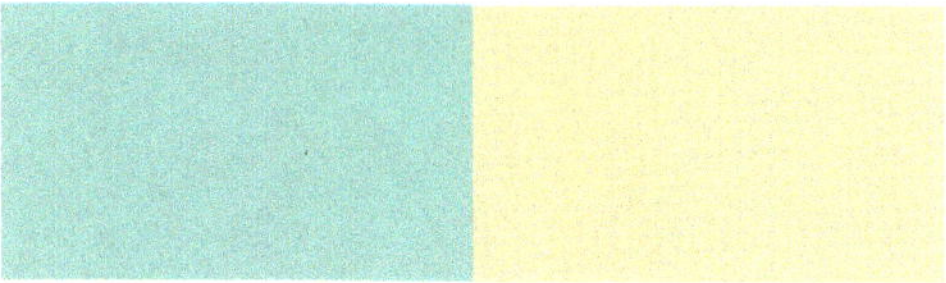

AQUAMARINE BEIGE

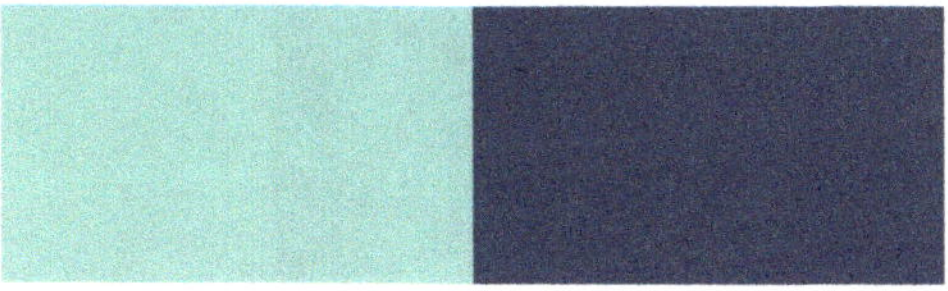

AQUAMARINE VIOLET BLUE

Aquamarine	Pearl White	Duke blue
Aquamarine	Citron Yellow	Blue Violet
Aquamarine	Mustard Yellow	Vinaceous Cinnamon
Aquamarine	Coffee	Cinnamon Buff

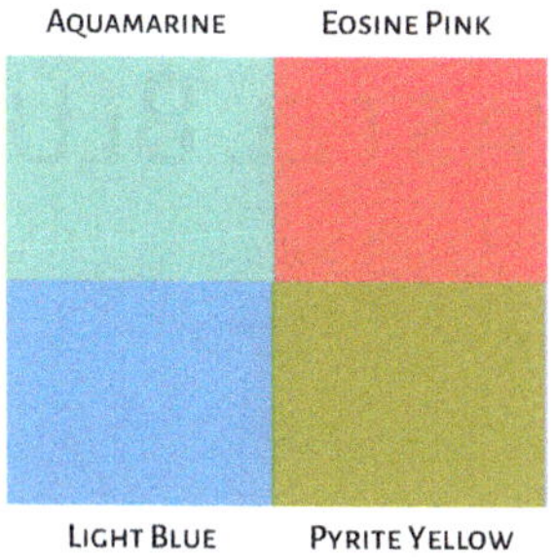
AQUAMARINE
EOSINE PINK
LIGHT BLUE
PYRITE YELLOW

PASTEL BLUE

#AEC6CF

RGB : 174. 198. 207

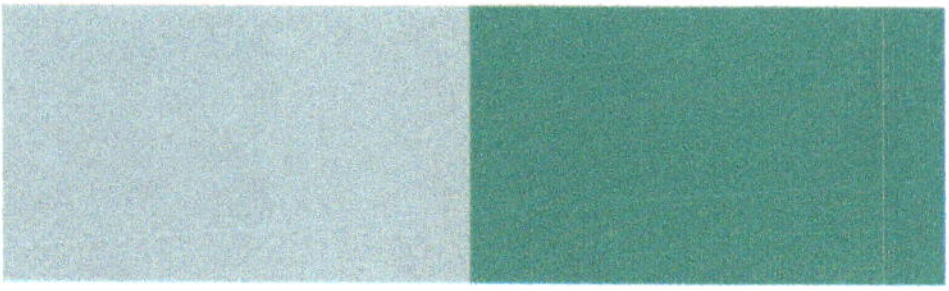

PASTEL BLUE PINE GREEN

PASTEL BLUE CHARTREUSE

PASTEL BLUE DARK BLUE

PASTEL BLUE | ETRUSCAN RED | CUTTLEFISH

PASTEL BLUE | GREEN BLUE | IVORY

PASTEL BLUE | PURPLE TRAFFIC | CINNAMON RUFOUS

PASTEL BLUE | CADET BLUE | PINK

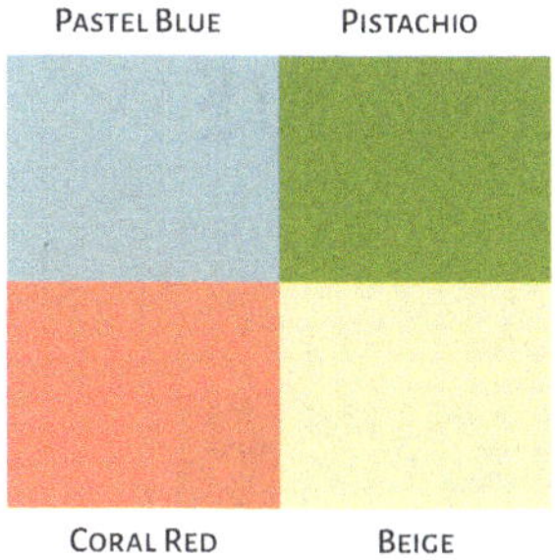
Pastel Blue
Pistachio
Coral Red
Beige

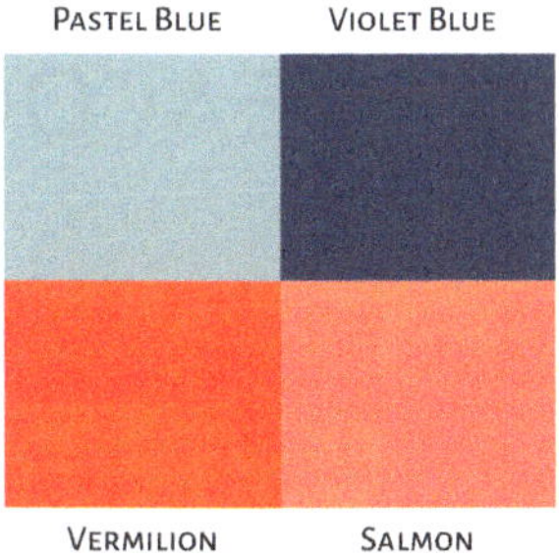
Pastel Blue
Violet Blue
Vermilion
Salmon

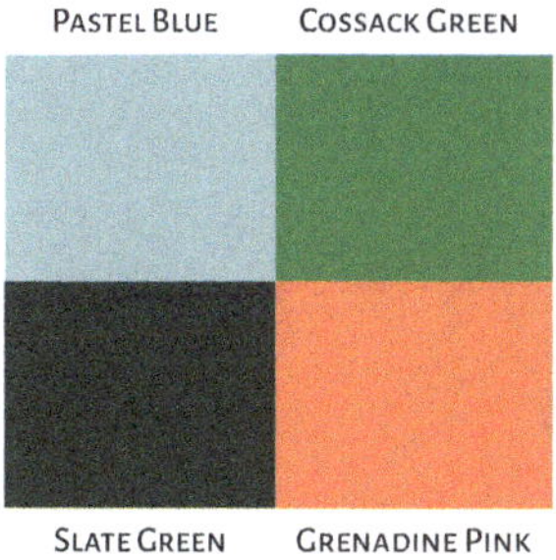
Pastel Blue
Cossack Green
Slate Green
Grenadine Pink

PEACOCK BLUE

#008789

RGB : 0. 135. 137

Peacock Blue Vermilion Bronze

Peacock Blue Sienna

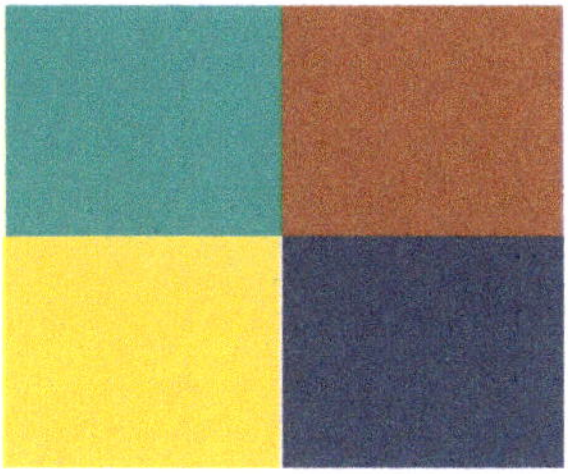

Gold Violet Blue

Antwarp Blue

#006880

RGB : 0. 104. 128

Antwarp Blue | Corn Snake

Antwarp Blue | Might Night Blue

Antwarp Blue | Gold

ANTWARP BLUE | PERSIAN ORANGE | JET BLACK

ANTWARP BLUE | TURQUOISE GREEN | MUSTARD YELLOW

ANTWARP BLUE | AUBERGINE PURPLE | CINNAMON RUFOUS

ANTWARP BLUE | GREEN BLUE | BEIGE

Antwarp Blue Eton Blue

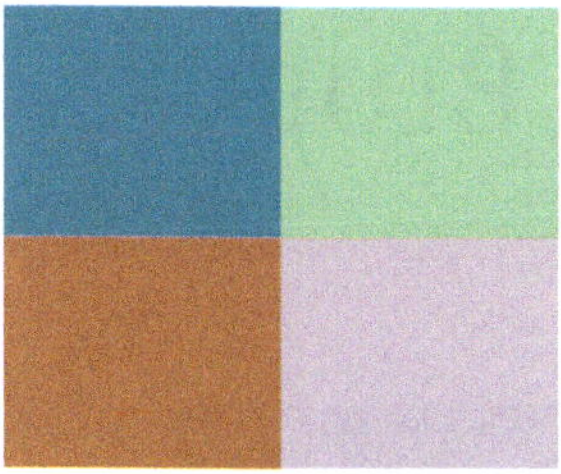

Corn Snake Thistle

Antwarp Blue Olive

Middle Yellow Red Pale Burnt Lake

Antwarp Blue Pine Green

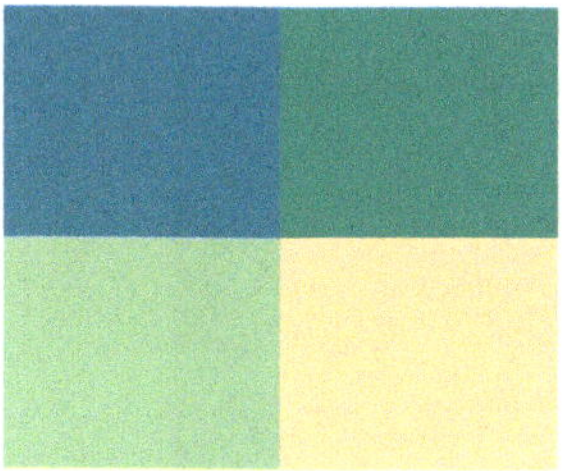

Mint Green Peach

Antwarp Blue Pistachio

Indian Lake Vinaceous Cinnamon

Antwarp Blue Pearl White

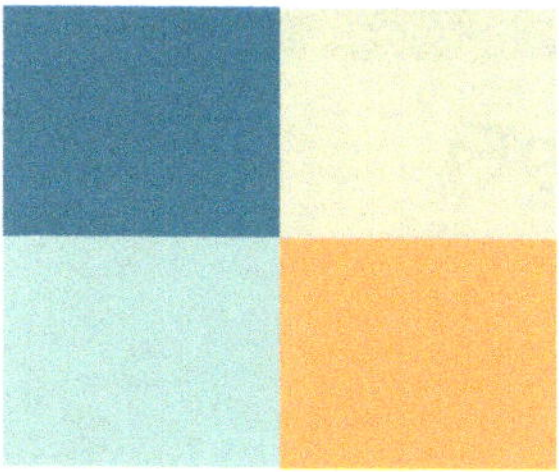

Nile Blue Cream Yellow

Antwarp Blue PapayaWhip

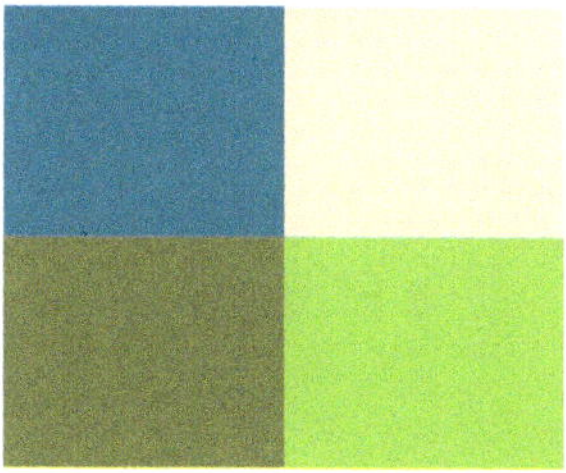

Olive Pale Green

Royal Blue

#4169E1

RGB : 65. 105. 225

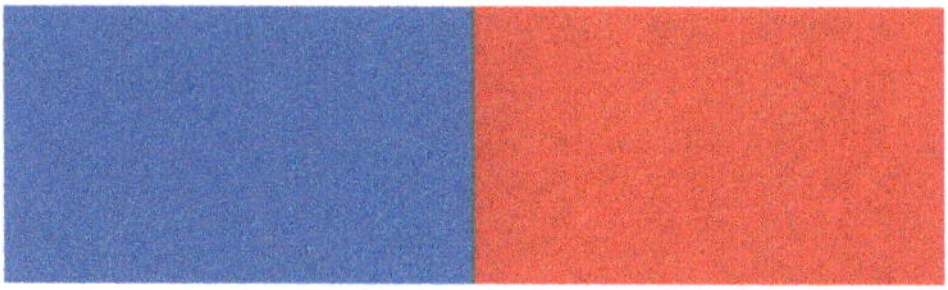

ROYAL BLUE RASPBERRY RED

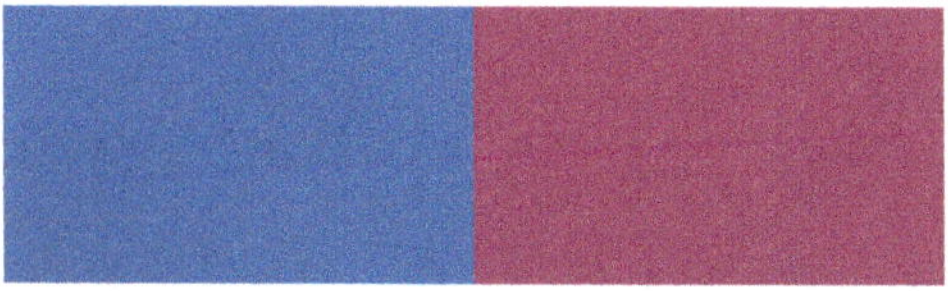

ROYAL BLUE PURPLE TRAFFIC

ROYAL BLUE BROWN MIDDLE YELLOW RED

ROYAL BLUE ACONITE VIOLET LAVENDER

ROYAL BLUE UCLA BLUE GRAYISH LAVENDER

ROYAL BLUE GRAY

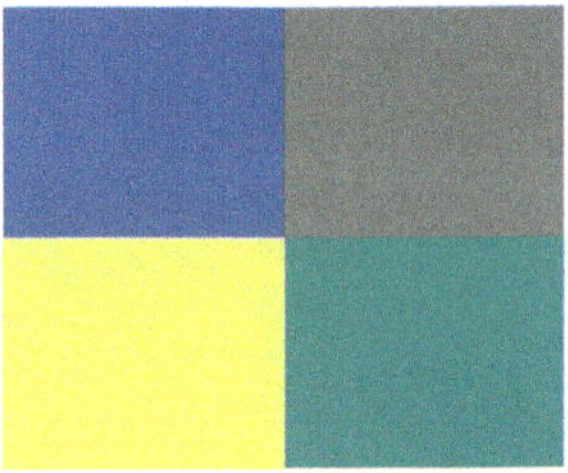

ICTERINE GREEN BLUE

ROYAL BLUE SIENNA

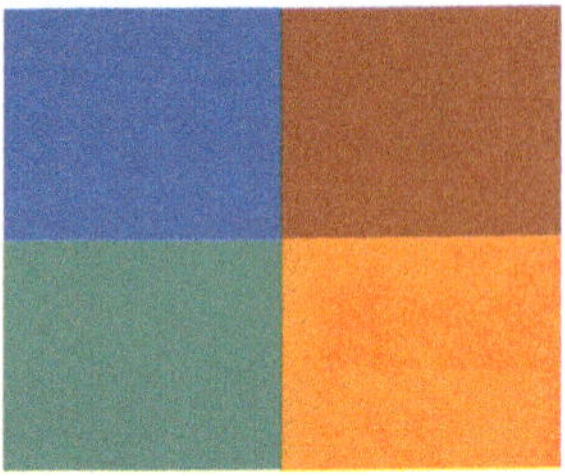

WINTERGREEN DREAM PUMPKIN COLOR

ROYAL BLUE LILAC

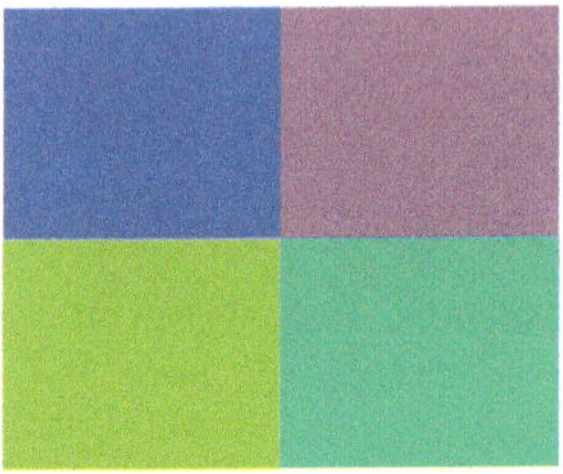

OLIVE YELLOW SEA GREEN

Navy Blue

#000080

RGB : 0. 0 128

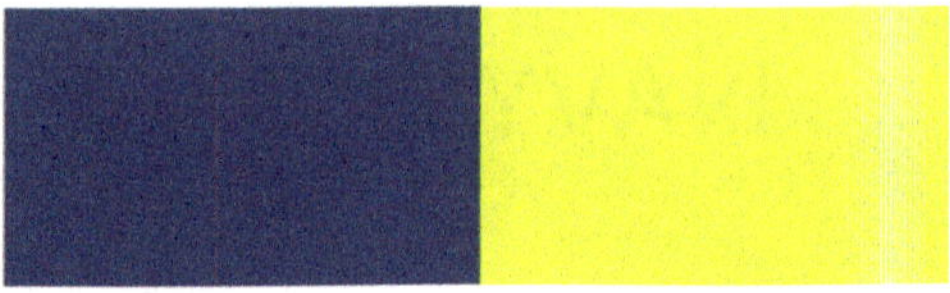

NAVY BLUE | YELLOW

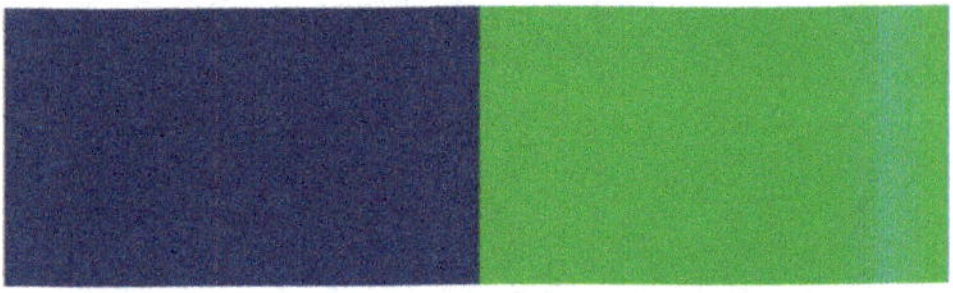

NAVY BLUE | DIAMINE GREEN

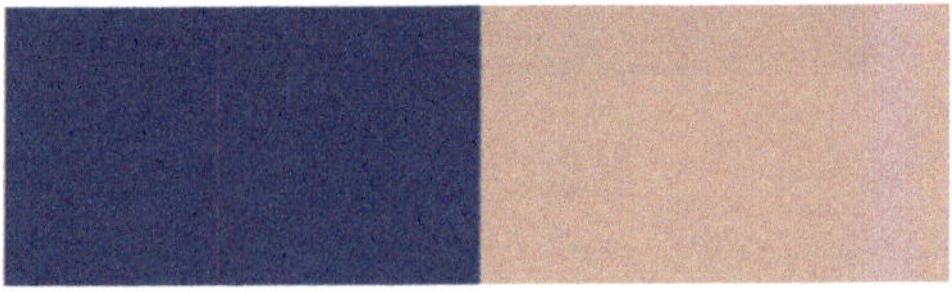

NAVY BLUE | CAMEO PINK

Navy Blue	Yellow Ocher	Ivory
Navy Blue	Red Orange	Persian Orange
Navy Blue	Amaranth	Greyish Beige
Navy Blue	Khaki	Purple

Navy Blue Bronze

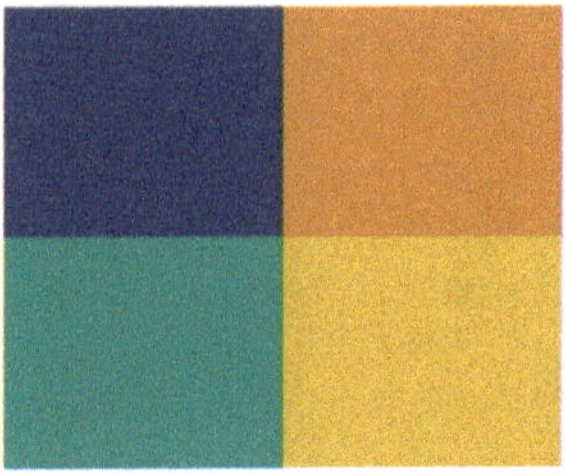

Pine Green Mustard Yellow

Navy Blue Cuttlefish

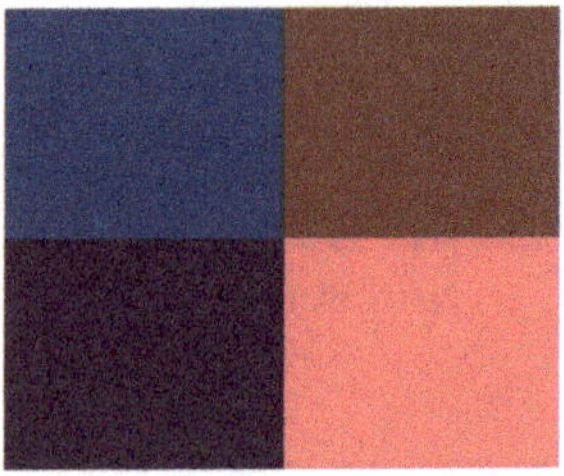

Dusky Madder Violet Eosine Pink

Navy Blue Cinnamon Buff

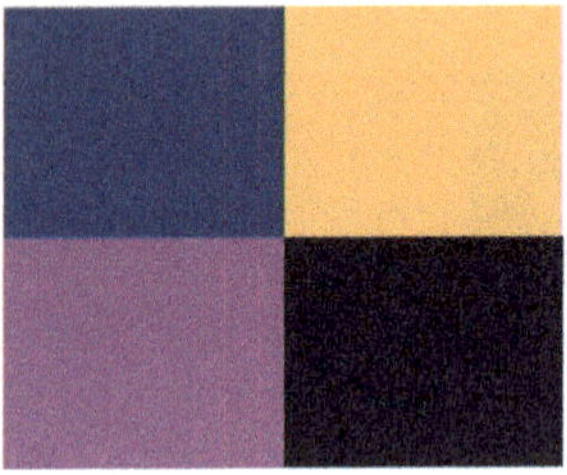

Aconite Violet Black

Duke blue

#001A57

RGB : 0. 26. 87

Duke blue	Cossack Green

Duke blue	Old Red

Duke blue	Beige	Pumpkin Color

Duke blue	Pearl White	Aquamarine

DUKE BLUE | ICTERINE | DEEP RUBY

DUKE BLUE | PINK ORANGE

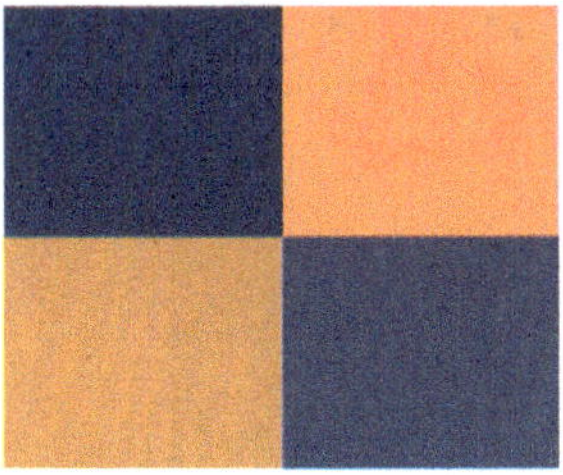

PERSIAN ORANGE | VIOLET BLUE

DUKE BLUE | IVORY

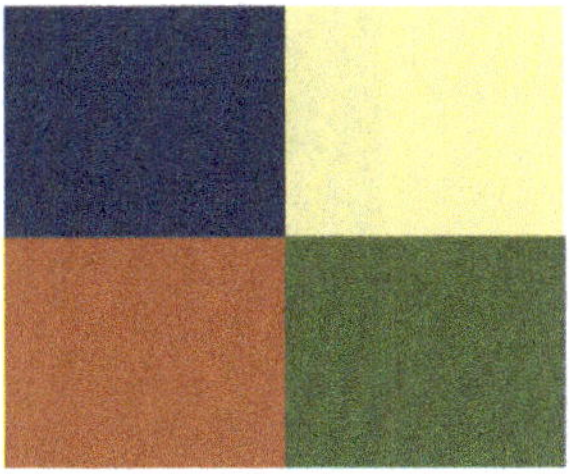

SIENNA | ARMY GREEN

Dark Blue

#182D3D

RGB : 24. 45. 61

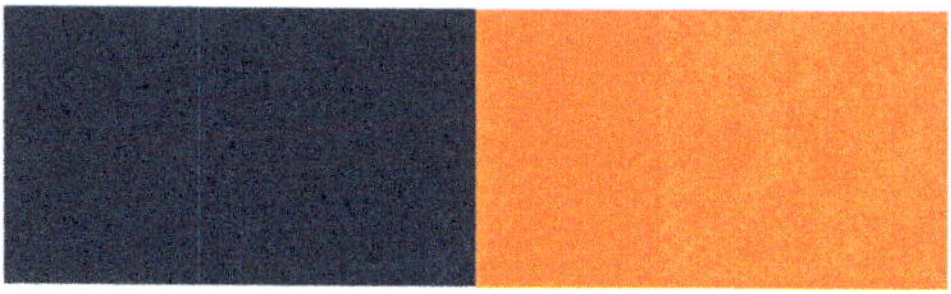

DARK BLUE PUMPKIN COLOR

DARK BLUE PEACH

DARK BLUE INDIGO BLUE

DARK BLUE PASTEL BLUE

DARK BLUE ORANGE PALE GREEN

DARK BLUE PISTACHIO

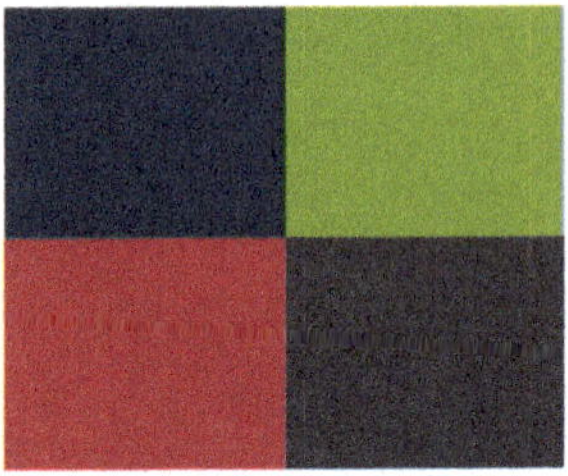

ROYAL RED JET BLACK

DARK BLUE PEARL WHITE

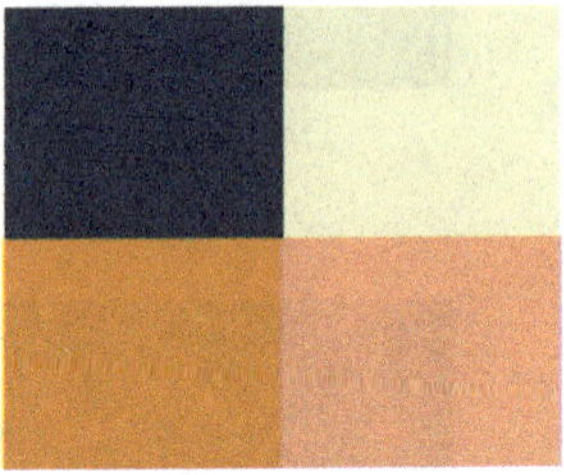

BRONZE VINACEOUS CINNAMON

WHITE

#FFFFFF

RGB : 255.255.255

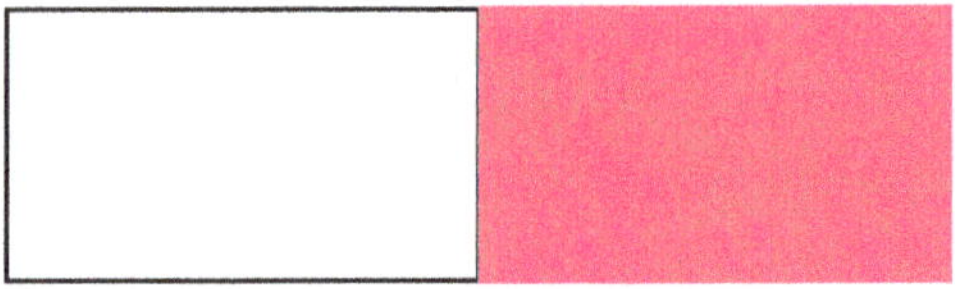

WHITE MAGENTA PINK

WHITE CHERRY AVOCADO

WHITE PUMPKIN COLOR

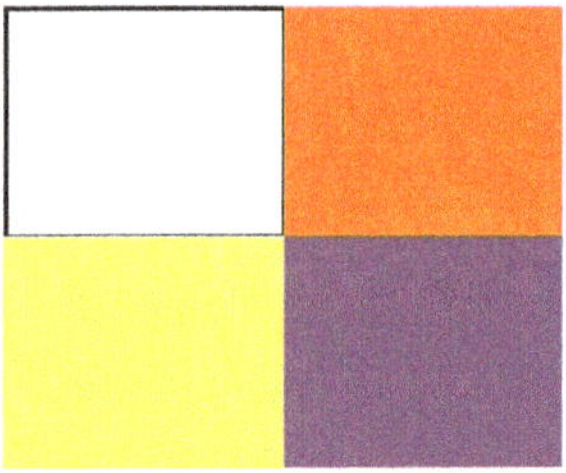

ICTERINE ACONITE BLUE

WHITE TOMATO

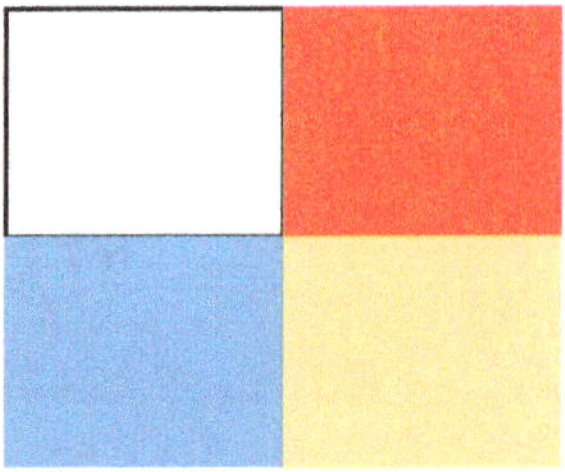

LIGHT BLUE PEACH

Beige

#F2E7BF

RGB : 242. 231. 191

Beige | Black

Beige | Aquamarine

Beige | Light Mauve

Beige | Royal Red

Beige	Chartreuse	Persian Orange
Beige	Alice Blue	Cossack Green
Beige	Pumpkin Color	Duke Blue
Beige	Green Blue	Antwarp Blue

Beige | Tile Color

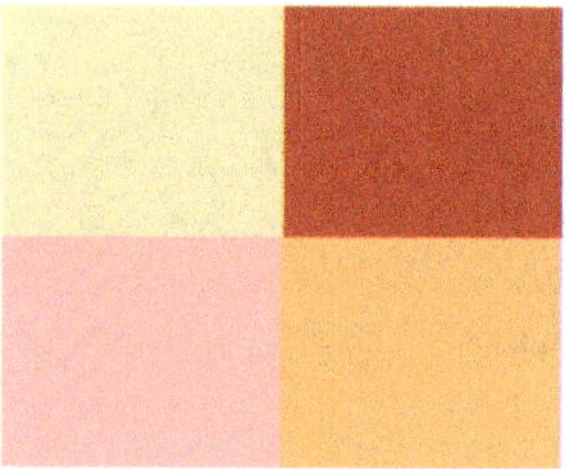

Rose Quartz | Cinnamon Buff

Beige | Olive

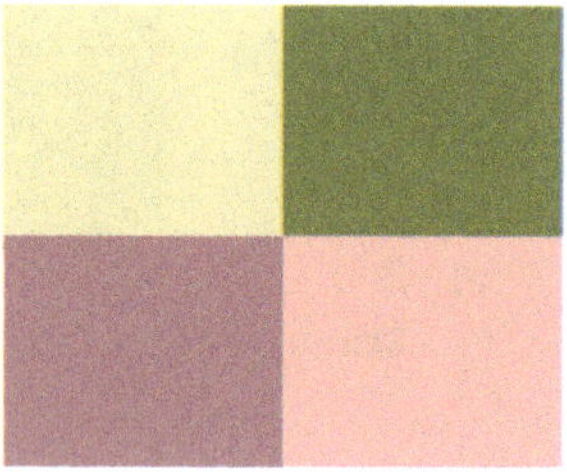

Laelia Pink | Rose Quartz

Beige | Old Red

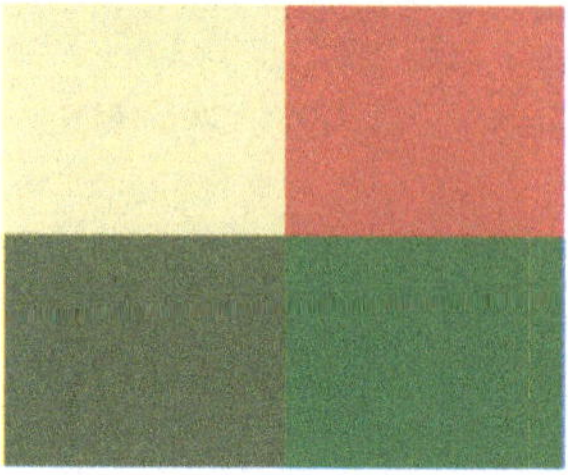

Olive Green | Cossack Green

Beige | Alice Blue

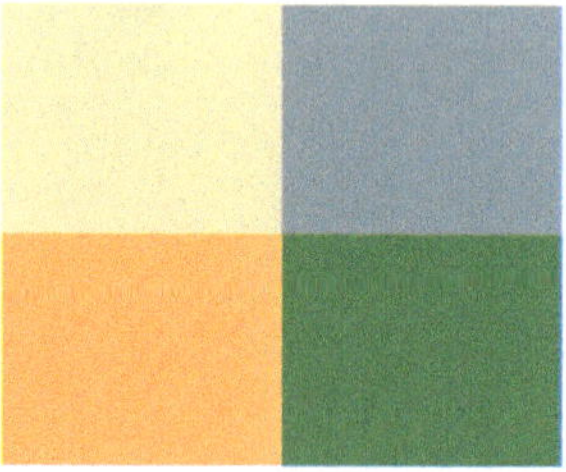

Cream Yellow | Cossack Green

Beige | Jet Black

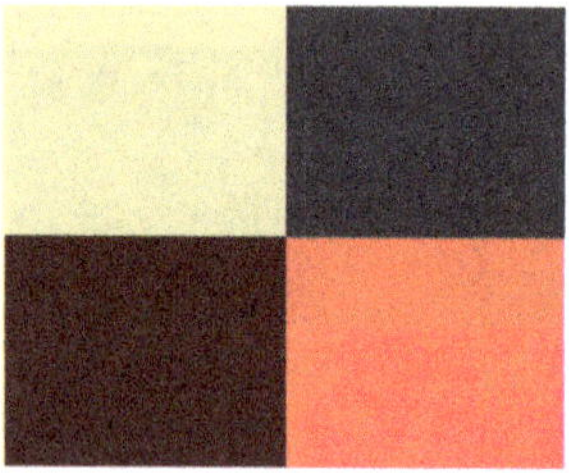

Coffee | Salmon

Beige | Olive

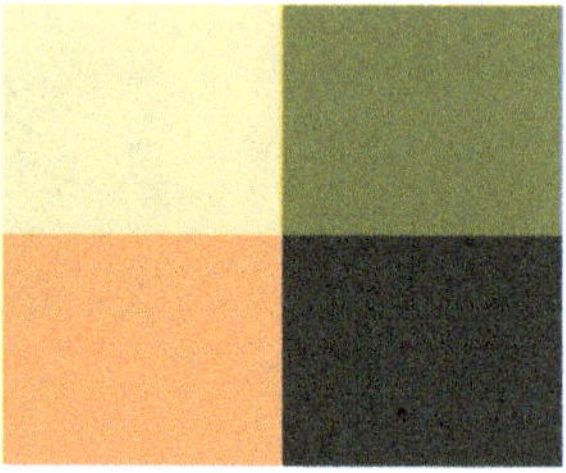

Middle Yellow Red | Slate Green

Beige Persian Orange

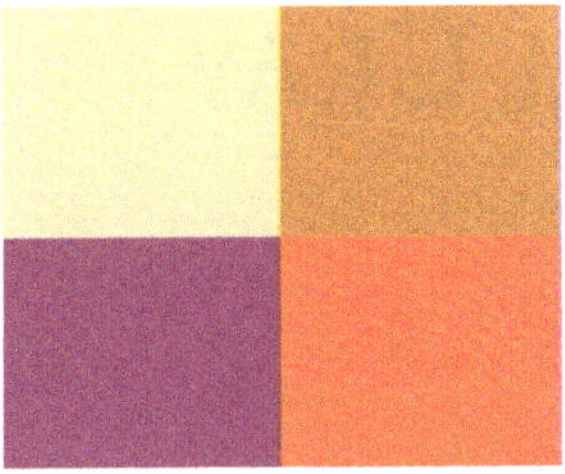

Fandango Grenadine Pink

Beige Pistachio

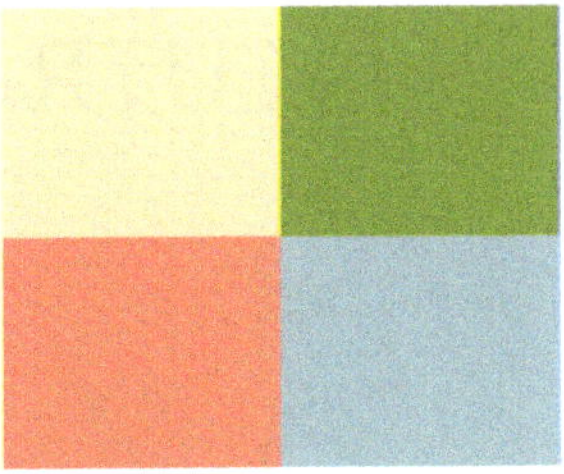

Coral Red Pastel Blue

Beige Alice Blue

Thistle Slate Green

Beige Pale Green

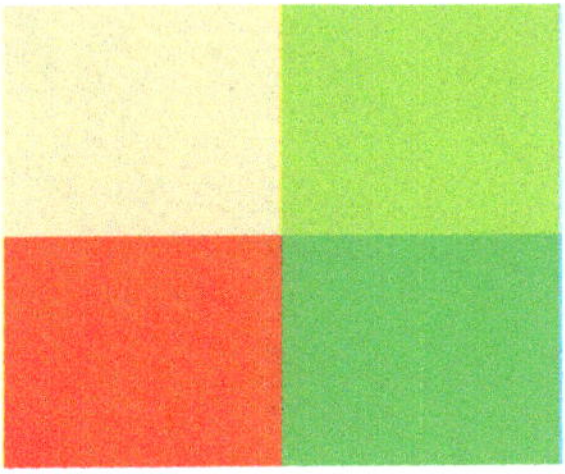

Almagre Malachite

Neutral Gray

#B0B8B5

RGB : 176. 184. 181

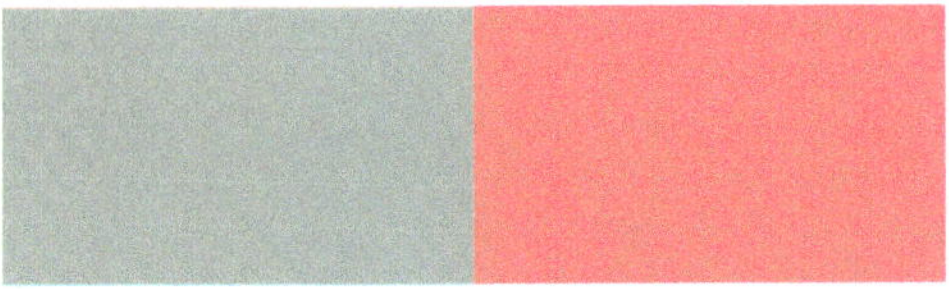

NEUTRAL GRAY — EOSINE PINK

NEUTRAL GRAY — DEEP INDIGO — ALICE BLUE

NEUTRAL GRAY — LIGHT MAUVE — CINNAMON BUFF

NEUTRAL GRAY — CHERRY — PEACH

NEUTRAL GRAY | AMETHYST | EOSINE PINK

NEUTRAL GRAY | ROYAL RED | BLACK

NEUTRAL GRAY | ROYAL RED | PEACH

NEUTRAL GRAY | SLATE GREEN | PERSIAN ORANGE

Neutral Gray Mahogany

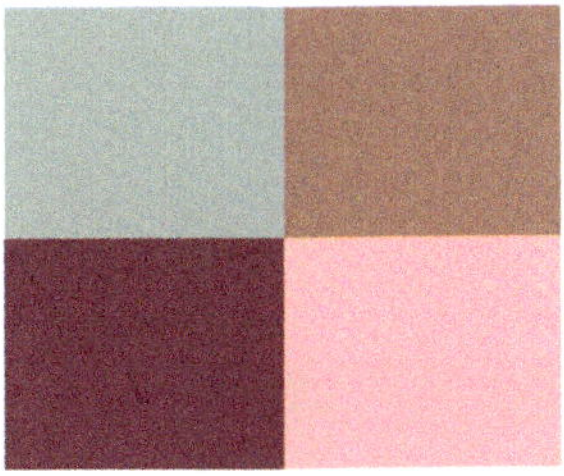

Pansy Purple Pink

Neutral Gray Almagre

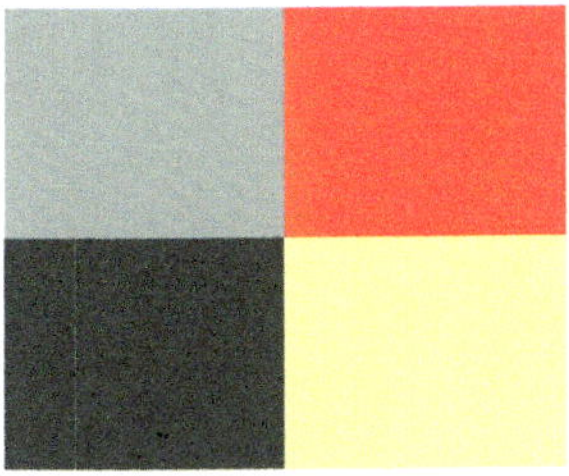

Slate Green Light Naples Yellow

Neutral Gray Indigo Blue

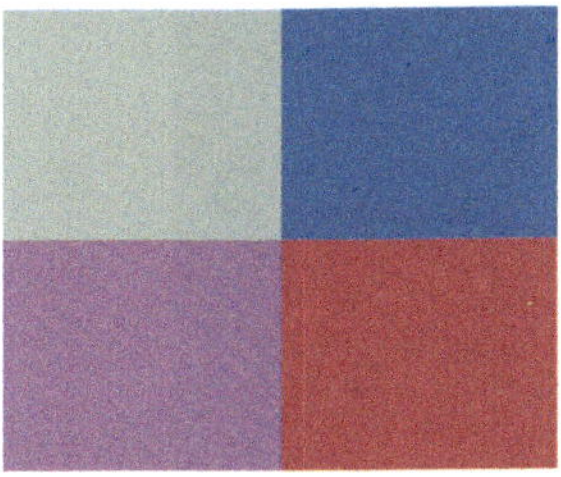

Aconite Violet Pompeian Red

Neutral Gray Black

Almagre Sea Green

Jet Black

#343434

RGB : 52. 52. 52

Jet Black Rose Quartz

Jet Black Bronze

Jet Black Taupe Brown

Jet Black Antwarp Blue Persian Orange

JET BLACK MINT GREEN TURQUOISE GREEN

JET BLACK IVORY

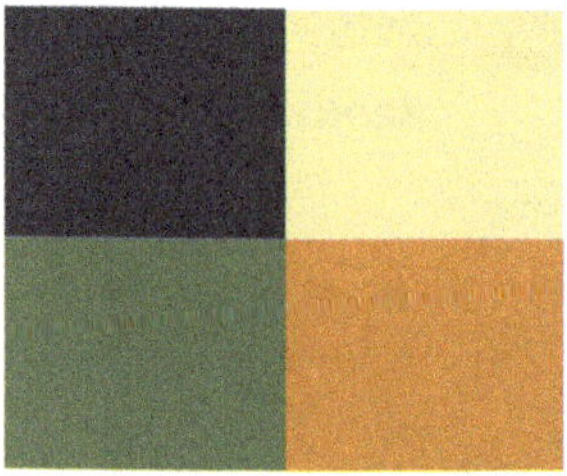

OLIVE GREEN BRONZE

JET BLACK PISTACHIO

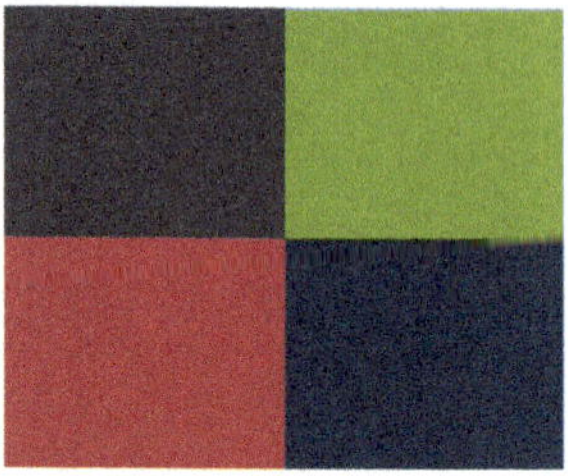

ROYAL RED DARK BLUE

Jet Black / Red

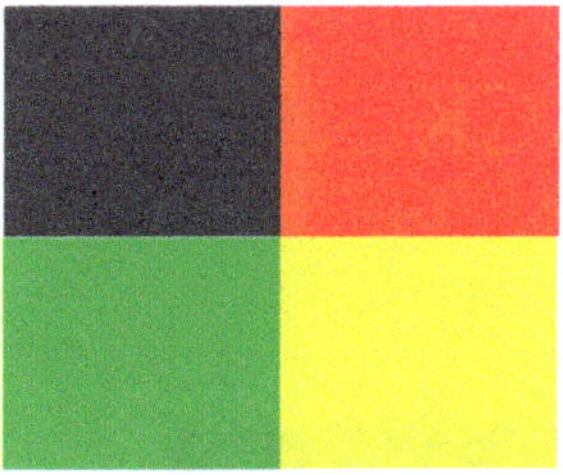

Diamine Green / Yellow

Jet Black / Pink Orange

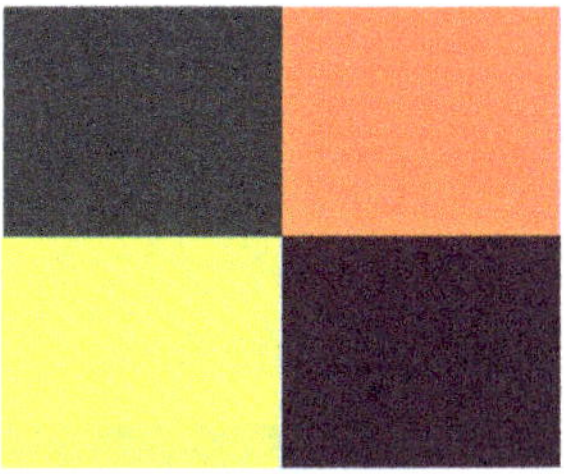

Icterine / Cotinga Purple

Jet Black / Sienna

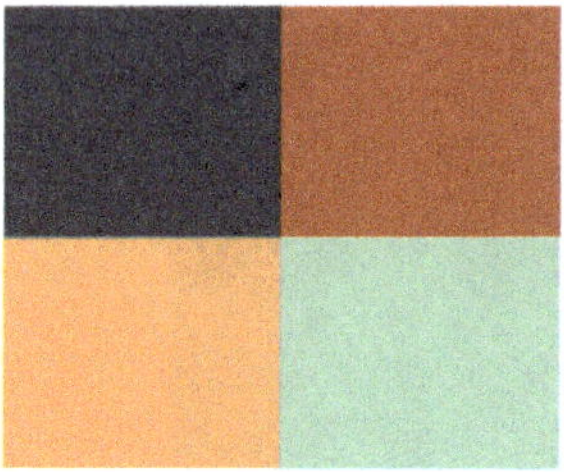

Middle Yellow Red / Turquoise Green

Jet Black / Beige

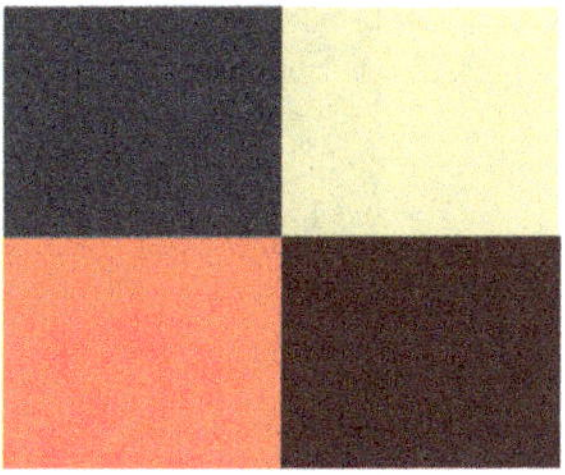

Salmon / Coffee

Jet Black / Cream Yellow

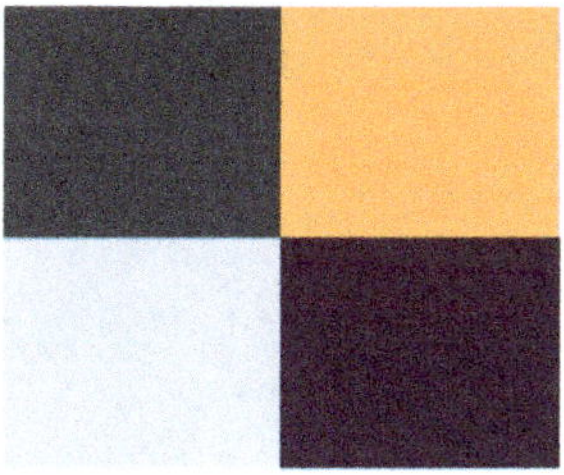

Lavender / Cotinga Purple

Jet Black / Violet

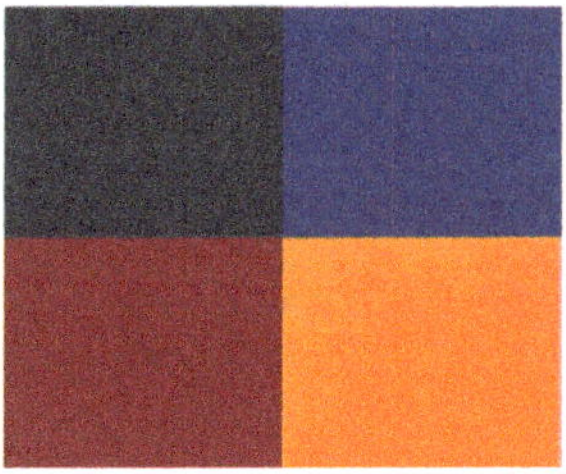

Burgundy / Pumpkin Color

BLACK

#000000

RGB : 0.0.0

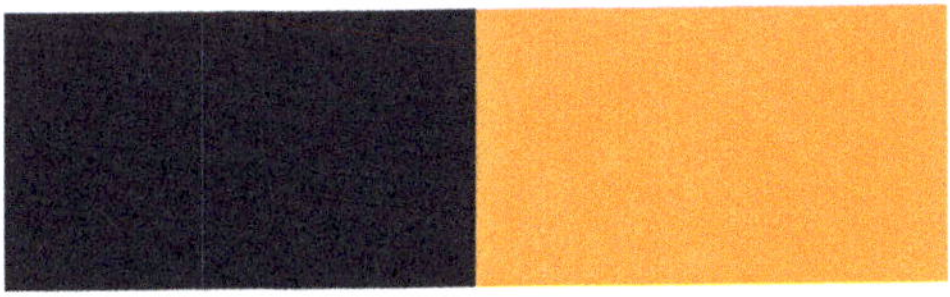

BLACK ORANGE

BLACK BEIGE

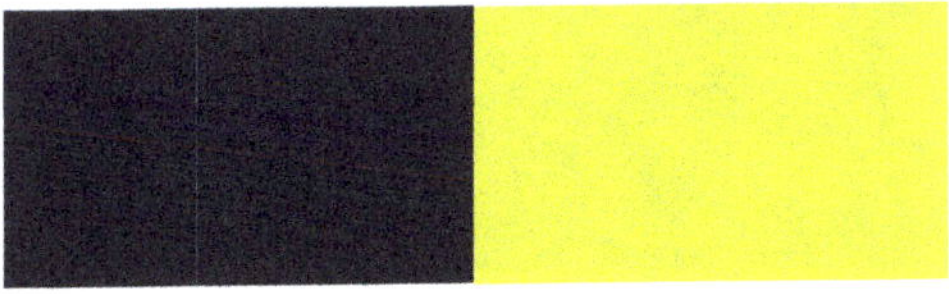

BLACK YELLOW

BLACK GRAY

Black Grenadine Pink

Black Raspberry Red

Black Lima

Black Vermilion Ivory

Black | Glaucous Green | Mahogany

Black | Green | Tomato

Black | Royal Red | Neutral Gray

Black | Orange | Purple Traffic

Black — Eosine Pink

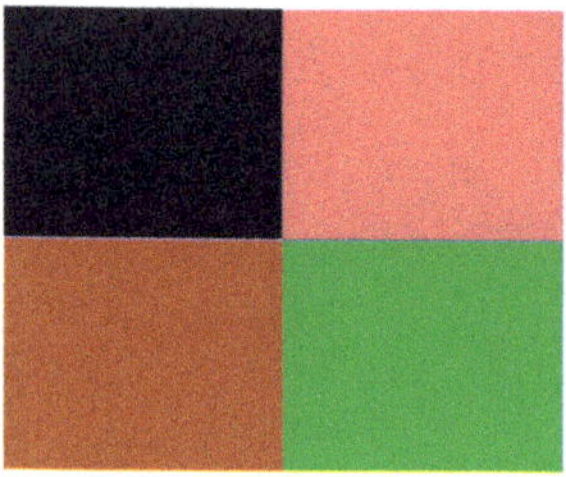

Sienna — Diamine Green

Black — Bronze

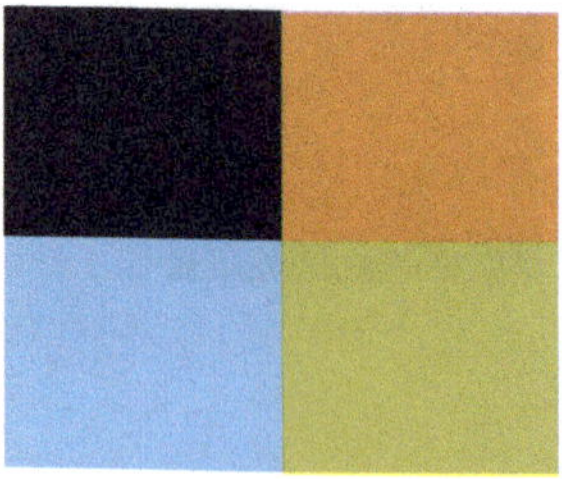

Light Blue — Pyrite Yellow

Black — Orange

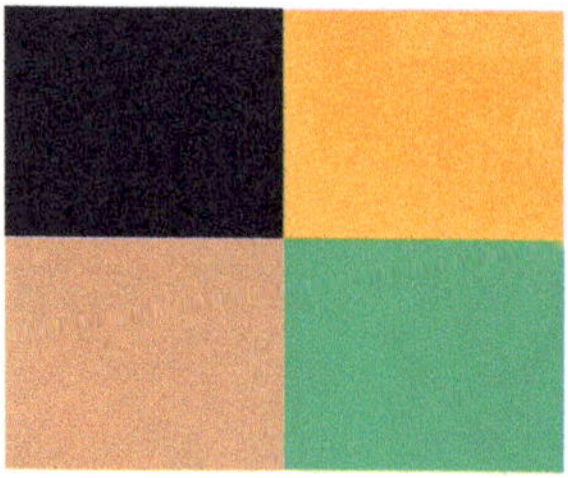

Vinaceous Cinnamon — Emerald Green

Black — Bronze

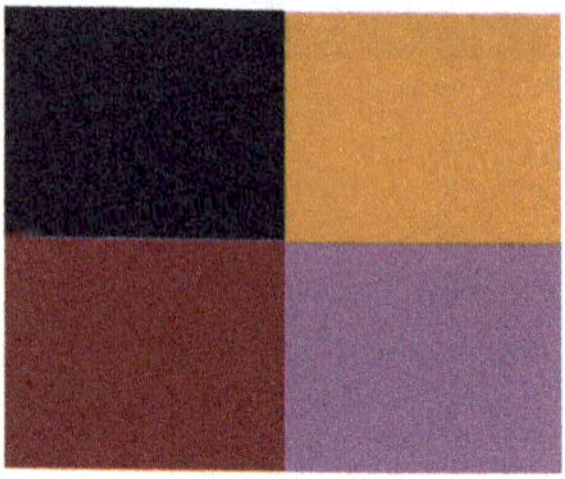

Pale Burnt Lake — Aconite Violet

Black — Eosine Pink

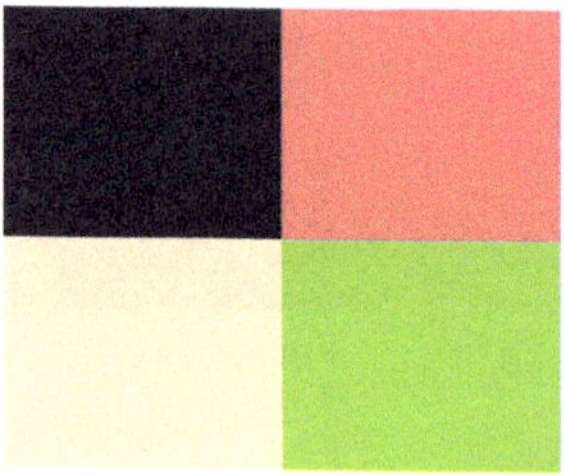

PapayaWhip — Pale Green

Black — Olive Brown

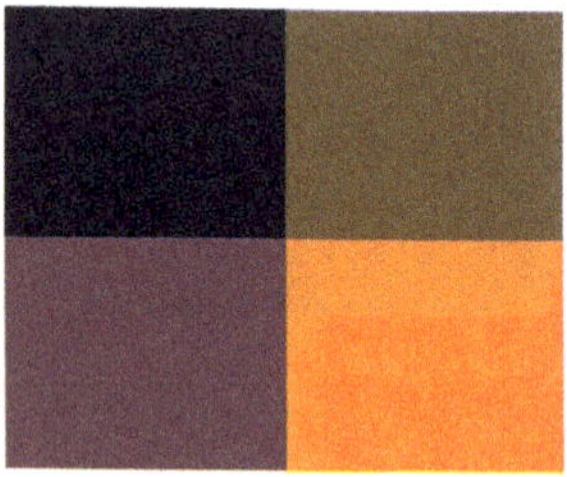

Taupe Brown — Pumpkin Color

Black | Bronze

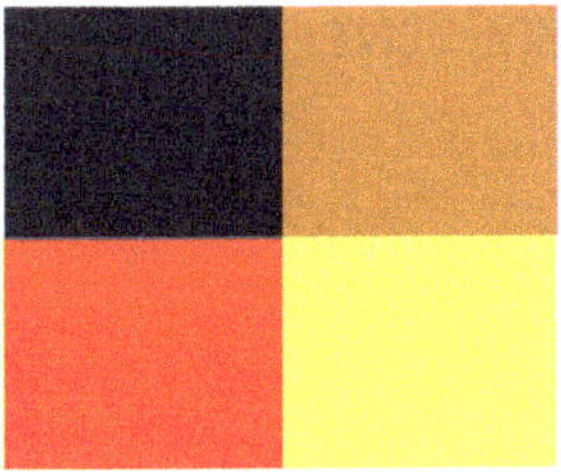

Almagre | Icterine

Black | Raspberry Red

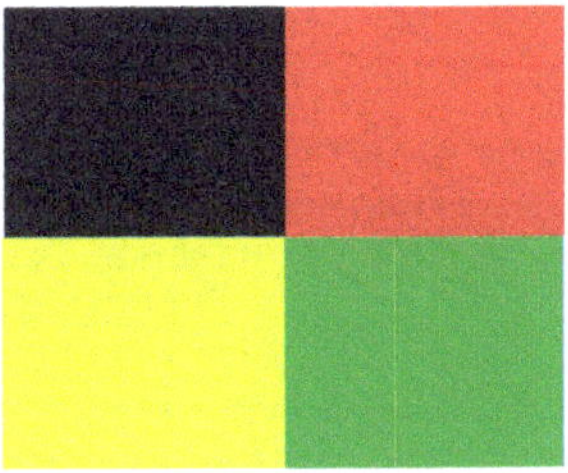

Yellow | Diamine Green

Black | Citron Yellow

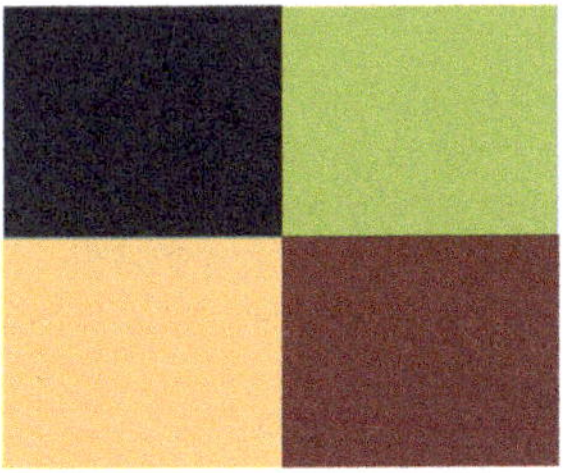

Cinnamon Buff | Madder Brown

Black | Violet Carmine

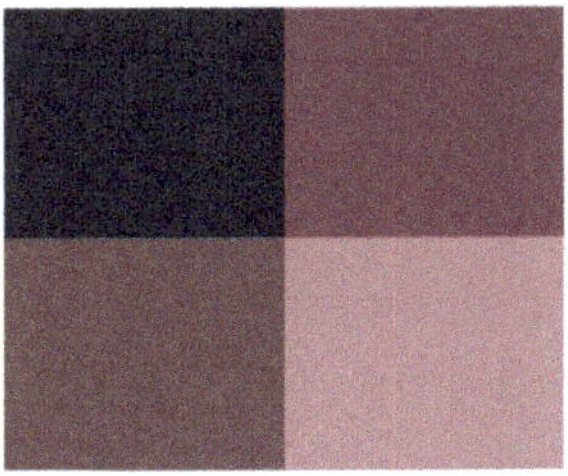

Vistoris Lake | Laelia Pink

Black | Sea Green

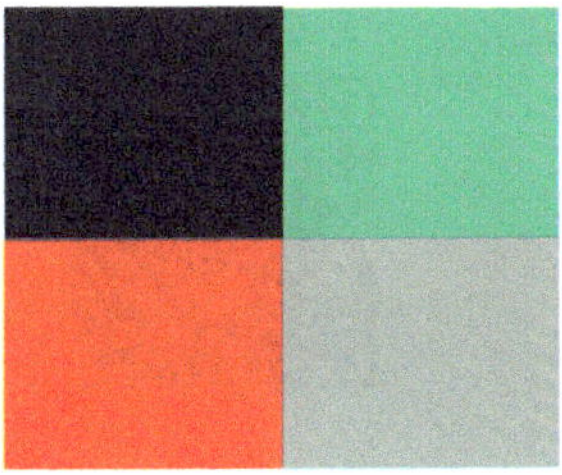

Almagre | Neutral Gray

Black | Aconite Violet

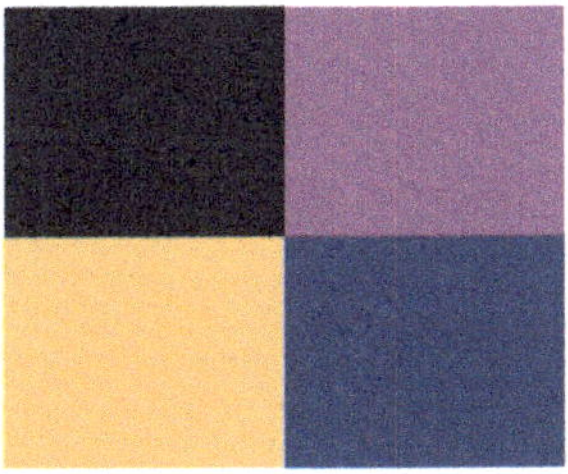

Cinnamon Buff | Navy Blue

EXCLUSIVE CONTENT

Thank you so much for choosing this book to accompany you in the wonderful world of colors. Each page has been crafted with care and dedication, with the hope that you enjoy and learn as much as we did while creating it.

Your interest and support are what make this project possible. If this book has inspired you, taught you something new, or simply proved useful, then we believe our work has been worthwhile.

As a token of our gratitude, we invite you to access exclusive content designed especially for buyers of the book.
How to access the exclusive content?

Scan the QR code below with your mobile phone.
Follow the instructions to access the exclusive content.
Or if you prefer, you can request it by sending an email to the following address, including your name and the words **"DICTIONARY II". Email: dimai.studio.sl@gmail.com**

It's that simple!

We would love to hear your thoughts on the book. If you enjoyed it, please consider leaving a review. Your feedback is very important to us.

QR Code for
Exclusive Content

Made in United States
Orlando, FL
14 July 2025

62946915R00115